Reviews for *That Book*
David Conley

A totally delightful, energetic and imaginative book. For lovers of the ancient world, young and old!

Ursula Dubosarsky, Author of over 50 books and Australian Children's Laureate 2020-2021

David Conley is a bigger legend than Odin and a bigger marvel than Marvel! He puts the Rock into Ragnarök and the Norse into Norsænivegavinnuverkfæraskúrinngullhringur!!!! This is how the Greeks would have illustrated their myths and legends and it's what the Norse gods really looked like! Trust me, I've asked them.

I loved reading his mythologies - though I had to build a wooden horse and hide inside it to sneak into my son's room to get the books off him to read them.

Dr Craig Cormick OAM, award-winning author of over 40 books for the young and young at heart.

Did you know that the ancient Egyptians worshipped a bin chicken-headed god? That talented Dave Conley knows this and many other Egypt-related stuffs and they're all here in this book! Jam-packed (did the Egyptians eat jam? I don't know, ask Dave Conley!) with more illustrations than the inside of Tutankhamun's tomb, this is a MUST READ for anybody interested in papyrus, embalming, sand and pointy triangle buildings.

Jol 'Bin Chicken' Temple,

50% of the pair of Kate and Jol Temple, critically acclaimed authors of lots of books I really like.

Whenever Terry and I take our time-travelling rubbish bin for a spin through the ancient mythical lands of Greece or Midgard, we always take David Conley as our guide- and if he's not available then we take one of his books. He's the most knowledgeable expert on Greek and Norse mythological figures we've ever met, and we've met them all!

Andy Griffiths, author of over 30 books including the critically acclaimed Treehouse series

That Book About Life Before Dinosaurs

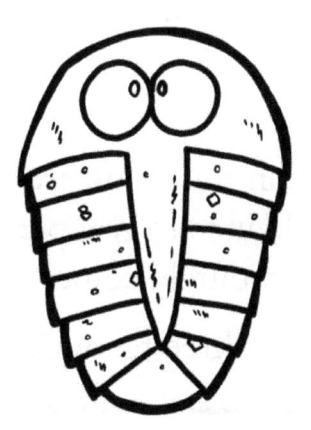

David Conley

First published 2024.

Copyright David Conley 2024.

The moral rights of the creator have been asserted.

All rights reserved. No part of this book may be reproduced or transmitted by a person or entity (including Google, Amazon or similar organisations), in any form or by any means, electronic or mechanical, including photocopying, recording, scanning, or by any information storage or retrieval system, without prior permission from the creator.

The characters in this book are fictitious and any resemblance to real persons, living or dead, is purely coincidental.

Dedicated to my three favourite people…

Contents

The Timeline Of Earth	1
The Hadean Eon	7
The Start Of Earth	9
The Archean Eon	11
Cracks In The Crust	14
The First Living Thing	17
Change	24
Prokaryotes	28
Cyanobacteria	34
When Earth Got Oxygen	36
The Proterozoic Eon	40
Tectonic Plates	44
The Great Oxygenation Event	47
Eukaryotes	50
Life On Land	54
Life Gets Complicated	56
The Ediacaran Period	59
Ediacaran Life	62
The Phanerozoic Eon	67
The Paleozoic Era	70
The Cambrian Period	72

The Cambrian Explosion	75
The Animals	78
Hallucigenia	80
Arthropods	82
Trilobites	85
Radiodonts	88
Chordates	94
Vertebrates	98
Land Plants	102
The End Of The Cambrian	104
The Ordovician Period	110
Lots Of Explosions	113
Molluscs	116
Cephalopods	121
Ostracoderms	128
Eurypterids	131
Water Levels Drop	136
The Silurian Period	139
Life Bounces Back	142
Silurian Eurypterids	148
Osteostracans	154
Life On Land	157
Jaws	166
Placoderms	169
The Spiny Sharks	172

Cartilaginous Fish	175
Bony Fish	177
The End Of The Silurian	181
The Devonian Period	184
Devonian Life	188
Arthrodira	193
Devonian Plants	202
Ray-Finned Fish	205
Elasmobranchs	208
Lobe-Finned Fish	211
Tetrapodomorphs	215
Tetrapods	220
The End Devonian Extinctions	225
The Carboniferous Period	231
Life In The Oceans	236
The Crustaceans	238
Elasmobranchs	240
Life In Rivers And Lakes	251
The Amphibians	259
The Amniotes	266
The Sauropsids	272
The Synapsids	274
The Land Arthropods	279
The Rainforest Collapse	283
The Permian Period	287

In The Oceans	290
Rivers And Lakes	294
The Amphibians	297
Sauropsid Skulls	304
The Parareptiles	307
The Eureptiles	315
The Synapsids	317
The Therapsids	323
The End Permian Mass Extinction	339
The Triassic Period	346
Living Things	348
Also By David Conley	358
Coming Up!	359
About The Author	360

The Timeline Of Earth

If we took a timeline from now and stretched it....

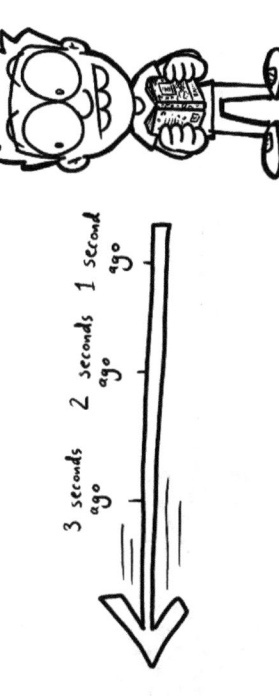

All the way back to when Earth first formed…

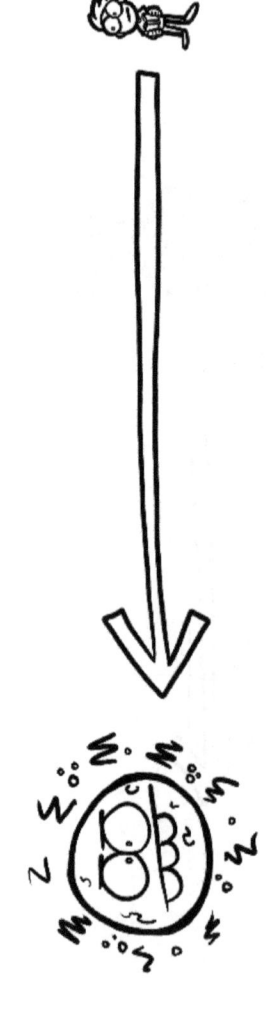

It would be 4.6 billion years long.

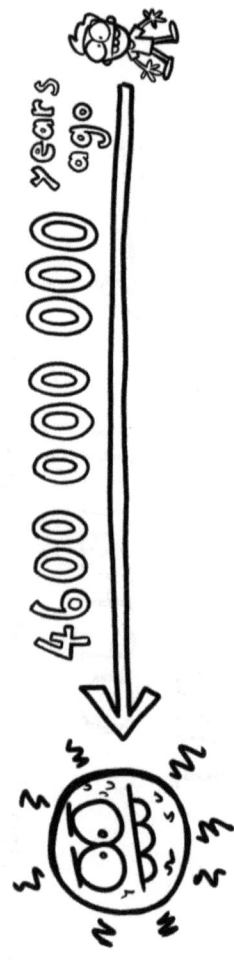

The timeline is chopped up into smaller chunks to make it easier to understand. Those chunks are eons, eras and periods.

The biggest chunks are the eons. There are four of them.

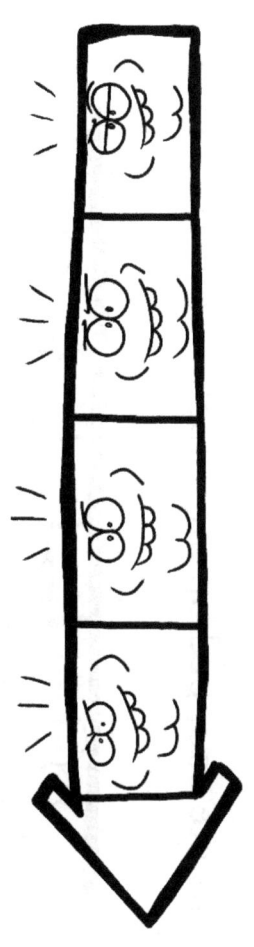

And the eons are chopped up into smaller chunks called eras.

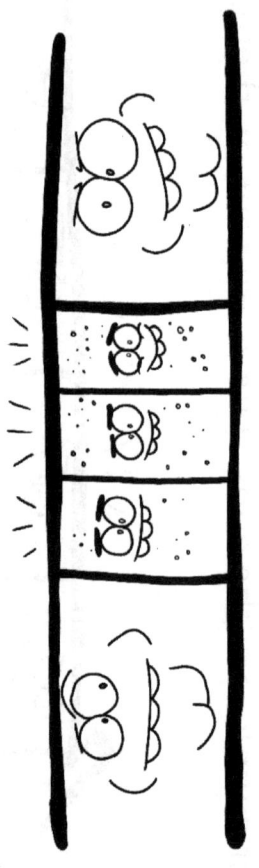

And eras are chopped into even smaller chunks called periods.

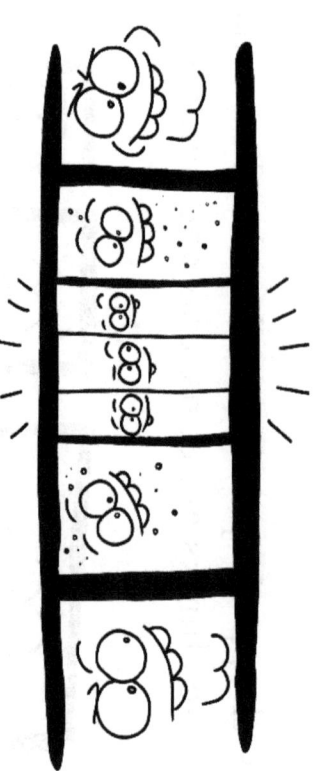

Now let's look at life before dinosaurs.

(You can turn the book back around the right way now.)

Let's start at the beginning with the very first eon.

It's time for…

THE HADEAN EON

The Hadean eon started about 4.6 billion years ago...

Lasted for 600 million years.

And it didn't have any eras or periods.

The Start Of Earth

Earth first formed 4.6 billion years ago as a hot ball of squishy lava and magma.

And it was covered in toxic gases like carbon dioxide and methane.

After 600 million years, Earth cooled down enough for the lava to become solid crust. And under the crust was a hot squishy layer of magma under the crust called the mantle.

Eventually it cooled down enough for oceans to form and the Hadean eon ended. It was time for...

THE ARCHEAN EON

The Archean eon started about 4 billion years ago…

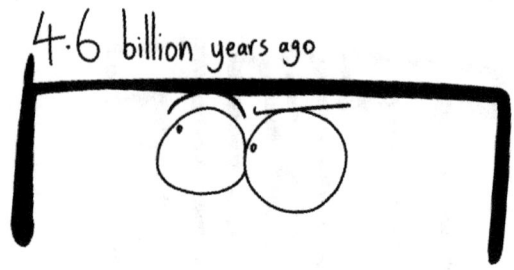

Lasted for 1.5 billion years.

And had four eras: the Neoarchean, Mesoarchean, Paleoarchean and Neoarchean.

During the Archean, Earth was mostly covered in oceans with a few chunks of land…

Cracks In The Crust

Earth got cracks in its crust almost as soon as it got a crust.

Lots and lots of cracks.

And they went from the top where the water was all the way down to the mantle.

Magma would go up the cracks…

Cook the water…

And make these things called hydrothermal vents. Hydrothermal vents are like underwater volcanos that shoot out hot water instead of lava.

The First Living Thing

Bubbling around in the hydrothermal vents were these things called nutrients.

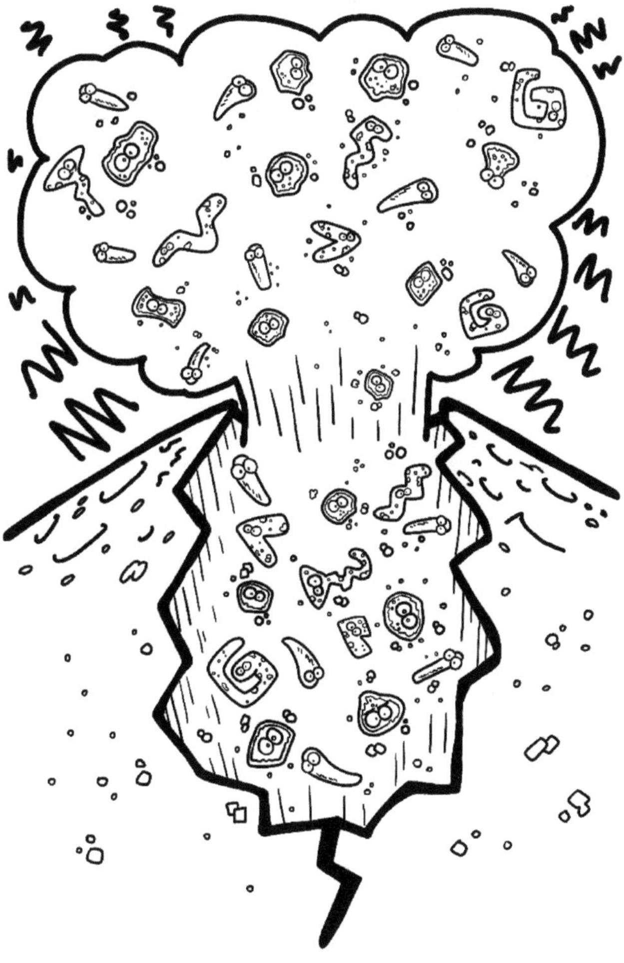

There were different types of nutrients.

They were all really, really small but they're also really, really important.

This nutrient is an amino acid.

There are lots and lots of different amino acids and they all do different things.

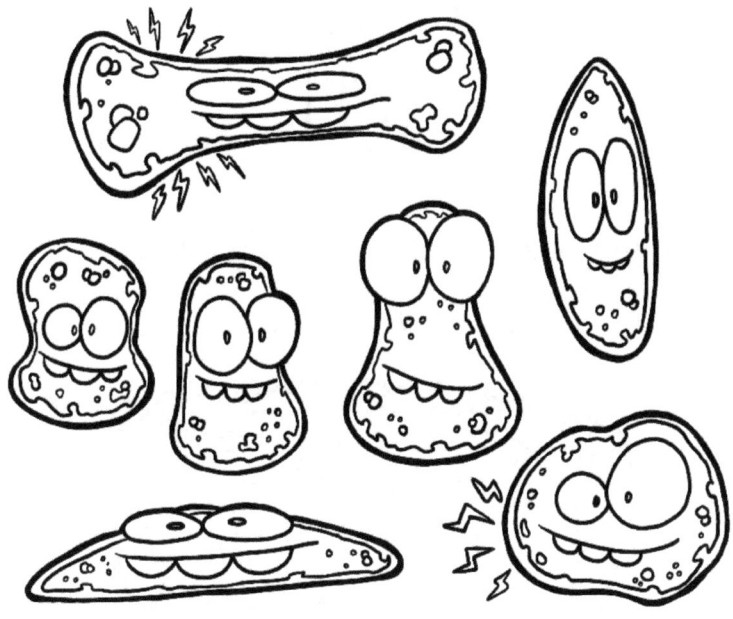

This nutrient is a lipid.

Lipids can store energy…

And get together to build big stuff.

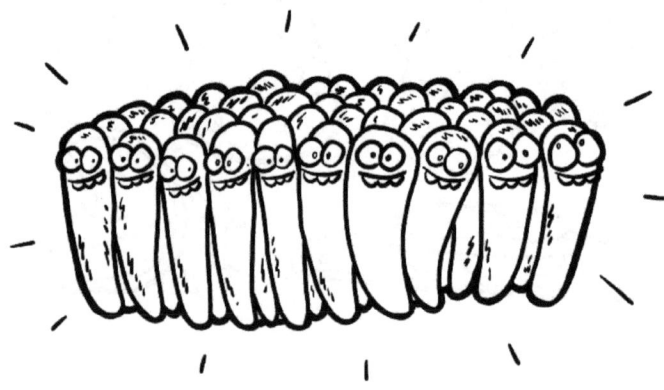

This nutrient is a protein.

Proteins fold into lots of different shapes and can do different things depending on how they are folded.

We're pretty sure, around 4 billion years ago, lots of amino acids, lipids and proteins got together around a hydrothermal vent…

Mixed together…

And made the first ever living thing.

Nobody really knows what the first living thing looked like.

But we do know it somehow got energy.

And it somehow made kids.

Change

Eventually life changed and there were lots of different living things.

When new types of living things pop up, we call that evolution ...

Evolution can happen in a whole population when something new spreads through the population over time.

Extinction is when a type of living thing dies and is gone forever.

When lots of different living things go extinct, we call that a mass extinction.

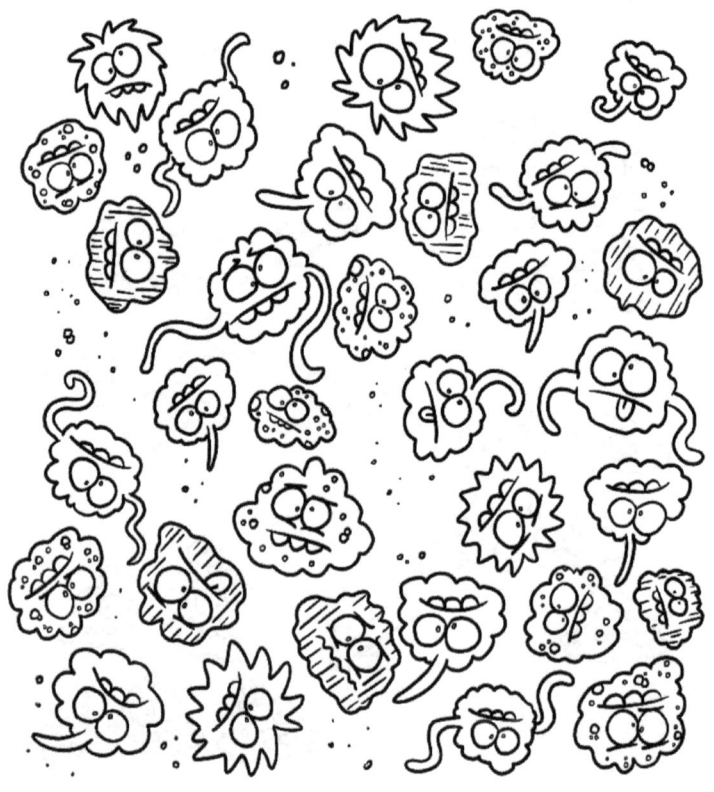

Evolution and extinction are the reasons life started as one type of living thing…

And ended up as the huge variety of different living things.

Prokaryotes

Near the start of the Archean eon, a new living thing evolved called a prokaryote.

Prokaryotes are really, really small…

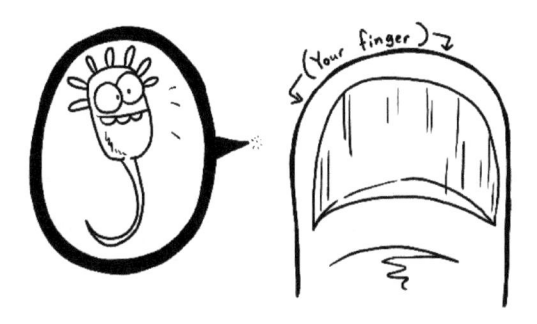

They're made of a blob (called a cell) and they have things called organelles in them.

Organelles do different jobs in the prokaryote to keep it alive.

There are two types of prokaryotes: bacteria and archaea.

Bacteria and archaea look almost exactly the same, but they do have differences…

Archaea are way tougher than bacteria. They can live in really hot areas that nothing else can survive.

Bacteria are not as tough but some of them have a trick when things get hard…

First, they just drop their extra bits off…

And go into a sort of hibernation as these things called endospores.

Until things finally aren't so bad anymore and they stop being endospores…

Grow back all their bits…

And get back to their lives.

Cyanobacteria

Sometime during the Archean this new prokaryote evolved. It was called cyanobacteria…

Cyanobacteria live in long chains of single cells all stuck together.

And they live on the top of the sea squished together in big carpets of slime.

When Earth Got Oxygen

This is oxygen. It's a gas.

You and I like oxygen because we breathe it.

But back in the Archean, there wasn't much oxygen at all. Earth just had lots of gases that would have killed us if we breathed them in.

One of the gases that was around was carbon dioxide. We do not breathe that in.

But then cyanobacteria evolved a new trick called photosynthesis.

Photosynthesis is when something breathes in carbon dioxide…

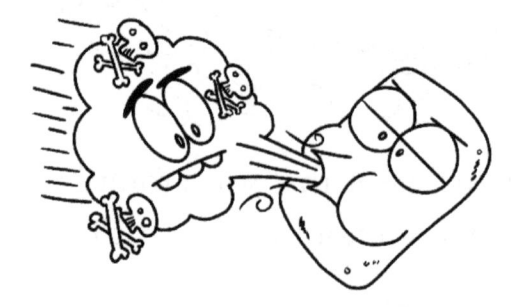

Then it messes around with it in its body…

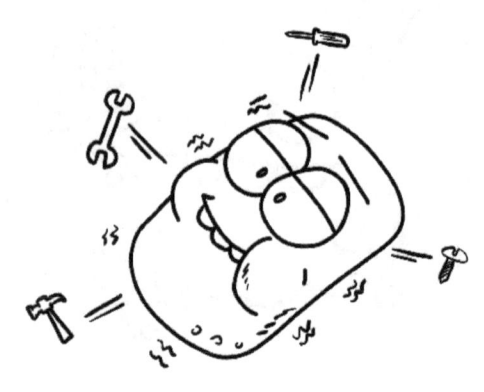

And breathes it out as oxygen.

We're not too sure when cyanobacteria started breathing oxygen out…

But about 2.5 billion years ago, there was so much oxygen building up on Earth that it ended the Archean Eon and started…

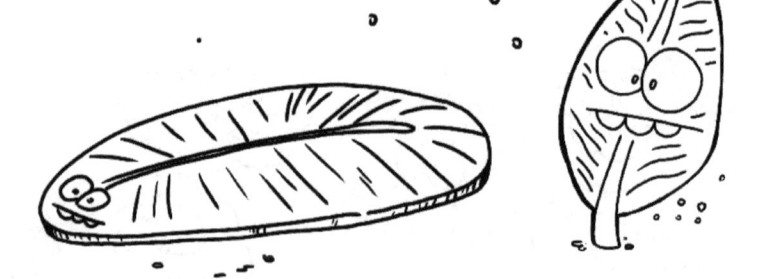

THE PROTEROZOIC EON

The Proterozoic eon was the third eon.

It started about 2.5 billion years ago…

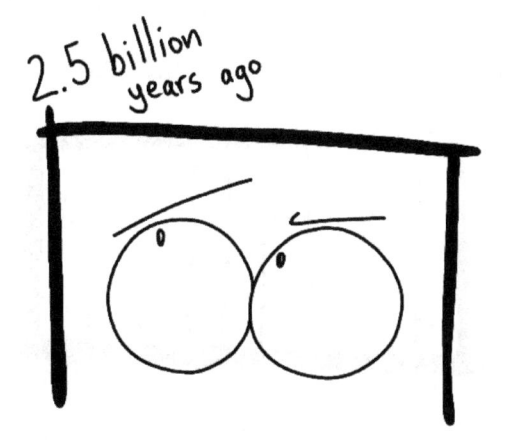

And lasted for 1.96 billion years.

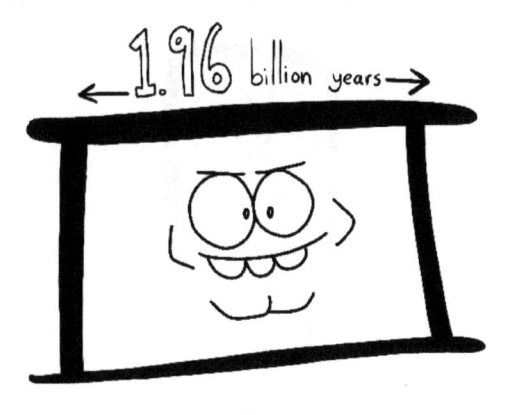

It had three eras: the Paleoproterozoic, the Mesoproterozoic and the Neoproterozoic.

And it had nine periods: the Siderian, Rhyacian, Orosirian, Statherian, Calmmian, Ectasian, Stenian and Ediacaran.

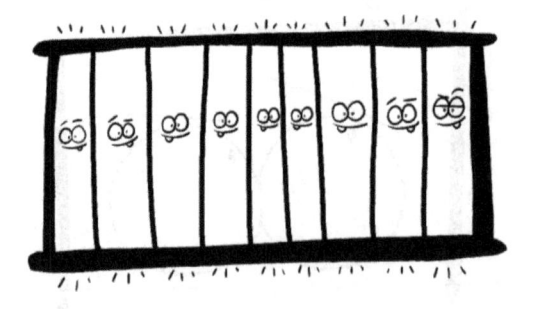

We'll look at the Ediacaran up close when we get to it. It had lots of great stuff in it.

During the Proterozoic eon, the chunks of land on Earth were bigger...

And near the start of the Proterozoic there may have even been this huge chunk of land called a supercontinent.

Tectonic Plates

Near the start of the Proterozoic eon, Earth's crust broke up into big pieces.

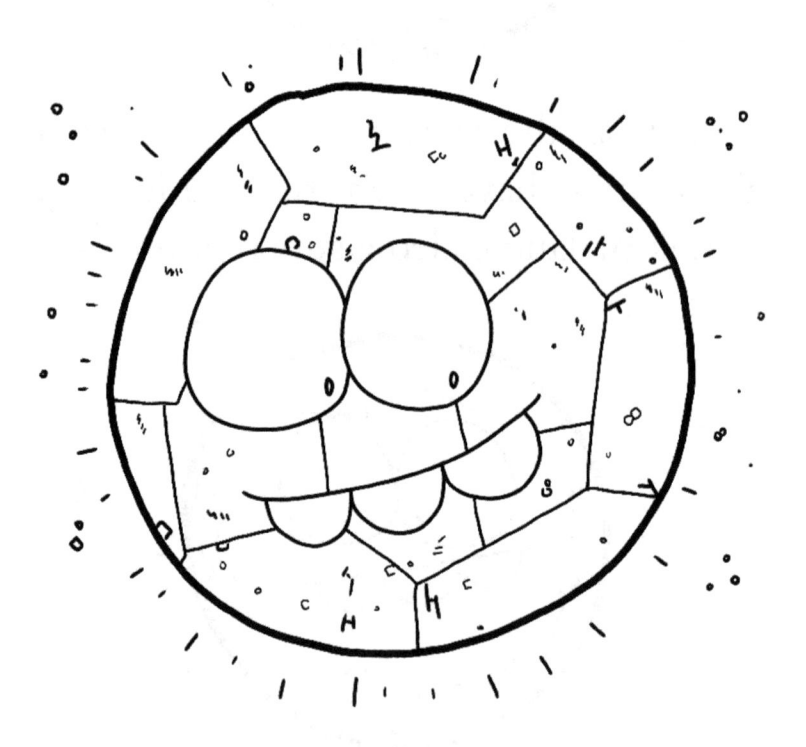

44

And those pieces (called tectonic plates) started sliding around.

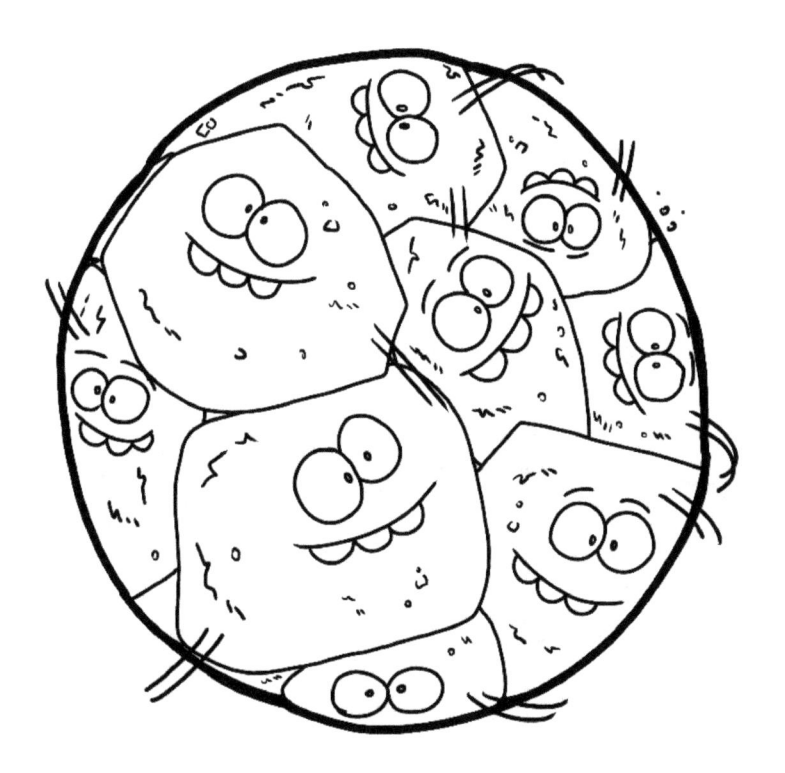

That's because they were floating on top of the mantle under them.

The plates rammed into each other…

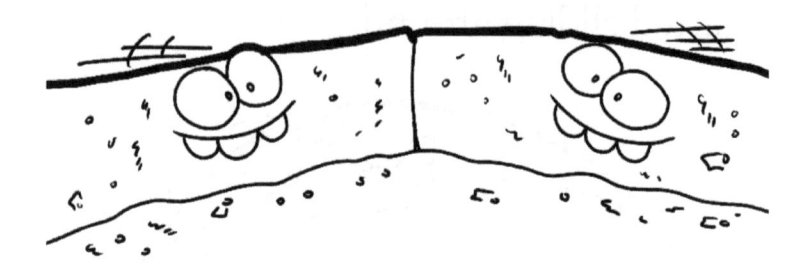

Pulled away from each other…

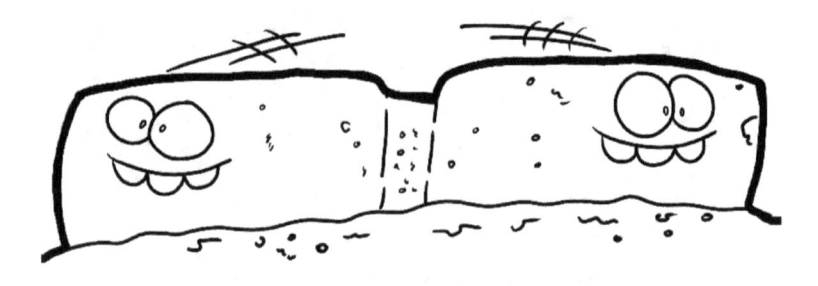

And rode over the top of each other.

The Great Oxygenation Event

Earth was building up more and more oxygen because of all the cyanobacteria making it...

But none of the prokaryotes had evolved to breathe oxygen in yet...

This means when they did breathe it in (because there was so much of it) ...

It killed them.

Because of all the oxygen on Earth, lots and lots of things died in Earth's first mass extinction. It was called the Great Oxygenation Event.

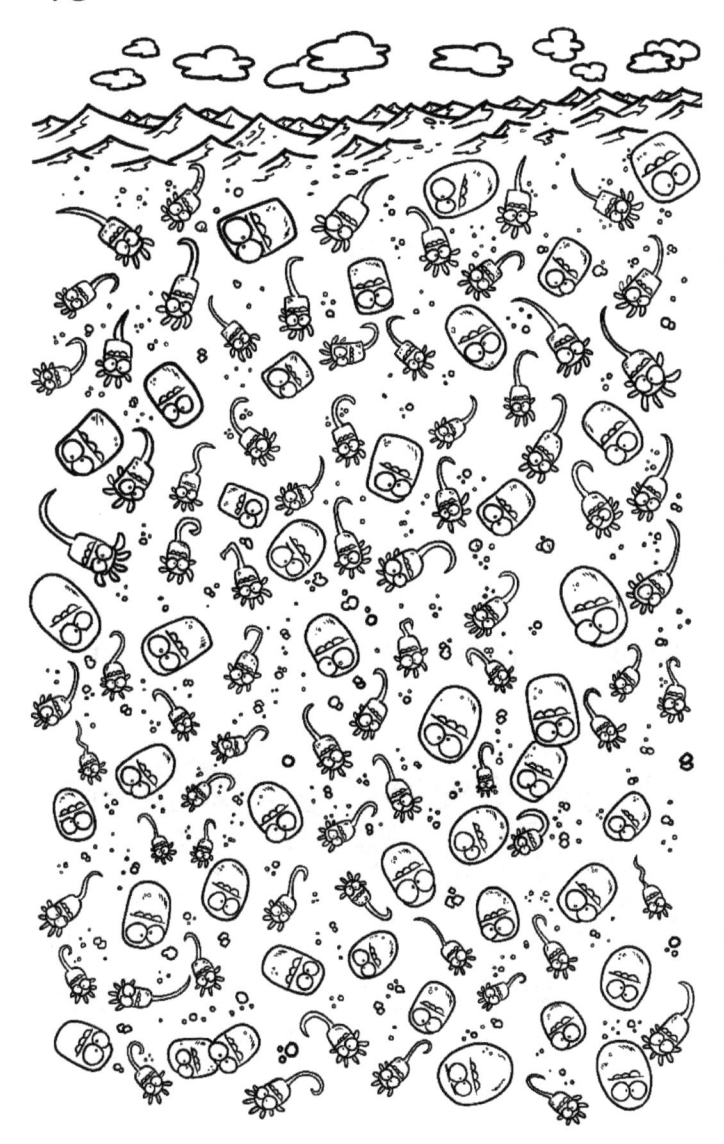

Eukaryotes

There were still a few prokaryotes left after the Great Oxygenation Event.

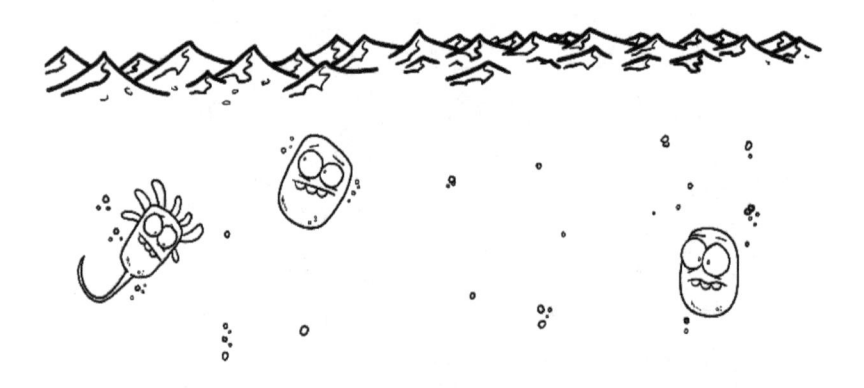

And slowly there were more and more.

And as life came back, this new type of life evolved about 2 billion years ago. It was called a eukaryote.

Prokaryotes and eukaryotes have a few differences but here's two of the big ones. First, eukaryotes can be about 50 times bigger than prokaryotes.

And second- prokaryotes have all their organelles floating around, but…

The organelles in a eukaryote are packed away in neat little blobs of their own.

And the most important stuff is all packed inside the biggest blob called a nucleus.

Life On Land

For a long time, there was lots of life in the water but none on the dry land.

54

Then sometime around the start of the Proterozoic eon, life started moving onto the land in the form of slime.

The slime could have been bacteria, archaea, cyanobacteria or even eukaryotes.

Life Gets Complicated

Some cyanobacteria and eukaryotes evolved to be multicellular (that means they have lots of cells in them) and all those cells were pretty much the same.

And for most of the Proterozoic eon, everything looked like slime or blobs (whether they were multicellular or not).

Then these new eukaryotes evolved. They were called animals.

Animals had lots of cells which had different jobs to each other.

Animals mark the start of the last period in the Proterozoic eon. It was…

THE EDIACARAN PERIOD

The Ediacaran period was the ninth and very last period in the Proterozoic eon…

It started about 635 million years ago…

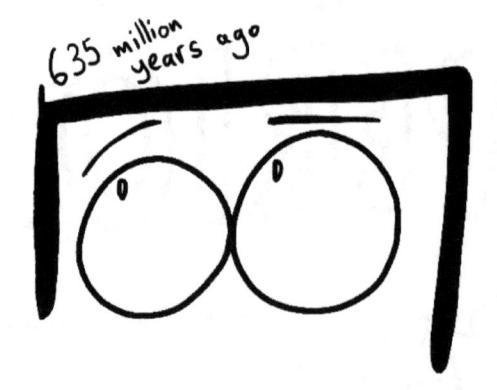

And it lasted for about 97 million years.

Earth had lots of big continents, but they were all down to the south of Earth.

In the north there were nearly all oceans.

Ediacaran Life

Lots of animals lived in the Ediacaran and spent their time sucking up all the slime and blobs floating around. Let's meet some of them...

This is Charnia. It was shaped like a big, squishy leaf and it could grow up to 2 metres tall (about as tall as a doorway).

Charnia were stuck to the bottom of the seafloor, and they ate any blob that floated into them.

This is Dickinsonia. It was built like a pancake and was about 1.5 metres long (that's about as long as an older kid).

Dickinsonia probably just slid around the seafloor sucking up the slime.

Kimberella was a bit like a clam. It had a shell, but the shell was really soft.

It was about 15 centimetres long (that's a bit longer than a regular pen).

And it probably slid around and ate slime, just like Dickinsonia.

About 539 million years ago, new animals evolved with hard bits…

They replaced the soft animals of the Ediacaran and ended the Proterozoic eon. It was the start of…

THE PHANEROZOIC EON

The Phanerozoic eon is the fourth eon in Earth's history.

It started about 538 million years ago…

And it's still going (so that means it's 538 million years long so far).

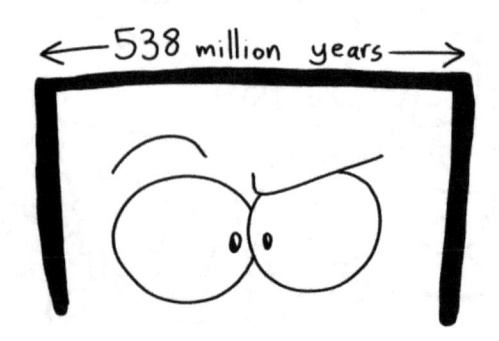

It's got three eras so far: Paleozoic, Mesozoic and Cenozoic...

And twelve periods: Cambrian, Ordovician, Silurian, Devonian, Carboniferous, Permian...

Triassic, Jurassic, Cretaceous, Paleogene, Neogene and Quaternary.

Now let's look more closely at...

THE PALEOZOIC ERA

The Paleozoic era started about 538 million years ago...

It lasted 286 million years.

And it's got six periods: the Cambrian, Ordovician, Silurian, Devonian, Carboniferous and the Permian.

THE CAMBRIAN PERIOD

The Cambrian period was the first period of the Paleozoic era.

It started about 538 million years ago…

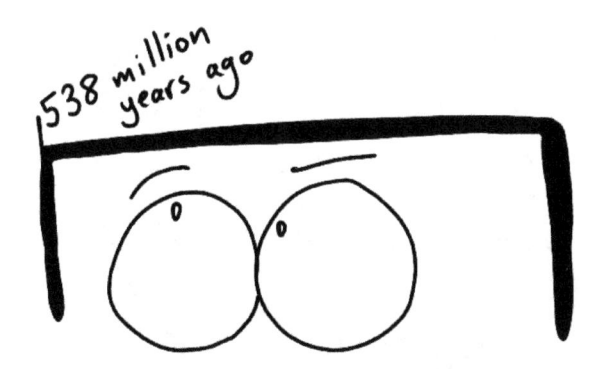

And it lasted for about 53 million years.

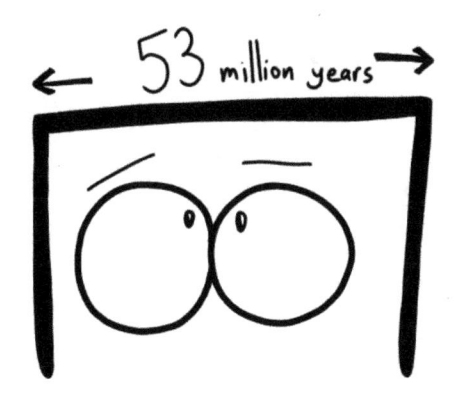

The continents were still in the south of Earth, but they were slowly moving north.

The Cambrian Explosion

The Cambrian period started with lots of new soft and hard animals evolving very quickly. That part of the Cambrian was called the Cambrian Explosion.

The evolution of hard bits and eyes probably caused the Cambrian Explosion (not the cartoon eyes I draw, these are REAL eyes).

Having hard bits meant animals could evolve lots of different types of shells, teeth, legs and tails.

And having eyes meant they could explore new areas…

Find other animals to eat…

And watch out for anything trying to eat them.

The Animals

There were lots of new hard and soft animals that evolved in the Cambrian…

Sea Anemones
Jellyfish
Brachiopods
Coral
Lots of wormy ones
Molluscs
Echinoderms

But we're going to ignore most of them…

And look at these two types of animals: arthropods and chordates.

Hallucigenia

This is Hallucigenia. It's not an arthropod or chordate but it's weird and cool.

It's so weird nobody was sure which way it went when they first found it.

Hallucigenia was about 5 centimetres long (that's about as long as an AA battery).

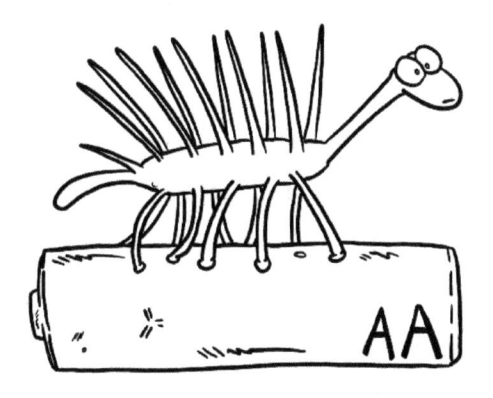

And it probably lived on the sea floor…

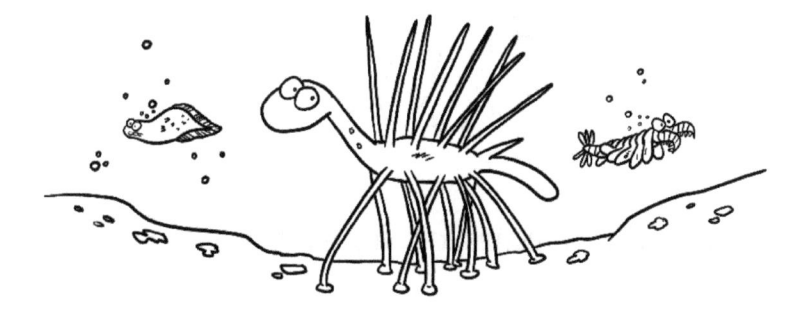

Eating anything that fit in its mouth.

Arthropods

Arthropods had hard stuff on the outside and soft stuff on the inside…

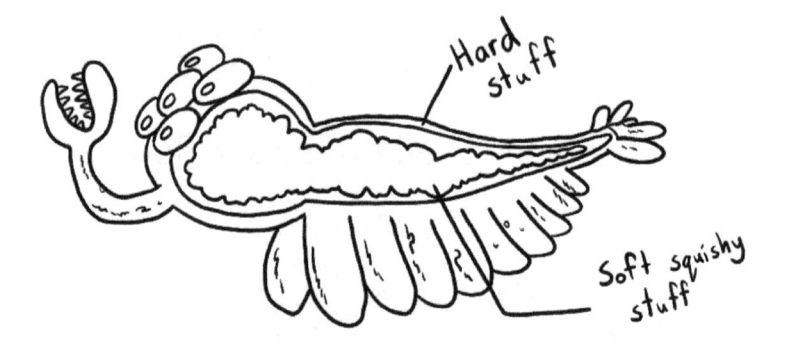

Hard stuff

Soft squishy stuff

They've got pairs of leggy things on their body…

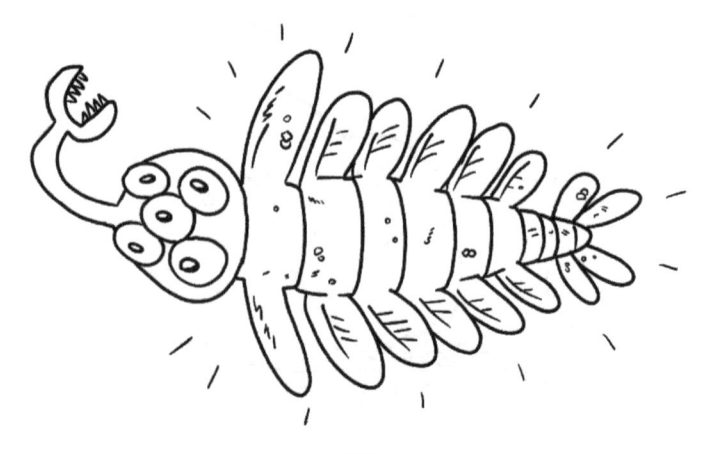

And bits of their bodies which look like they've been copied over and over.

There were lots of different arthropods. They dominated life in the Cambrian.

But we're going to ignore most of them...

And look at these two types of arthropods: trilobites and radiodonts.

Trilobites

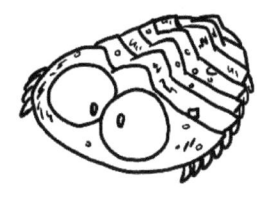

There were lots of really different types of trilobites.

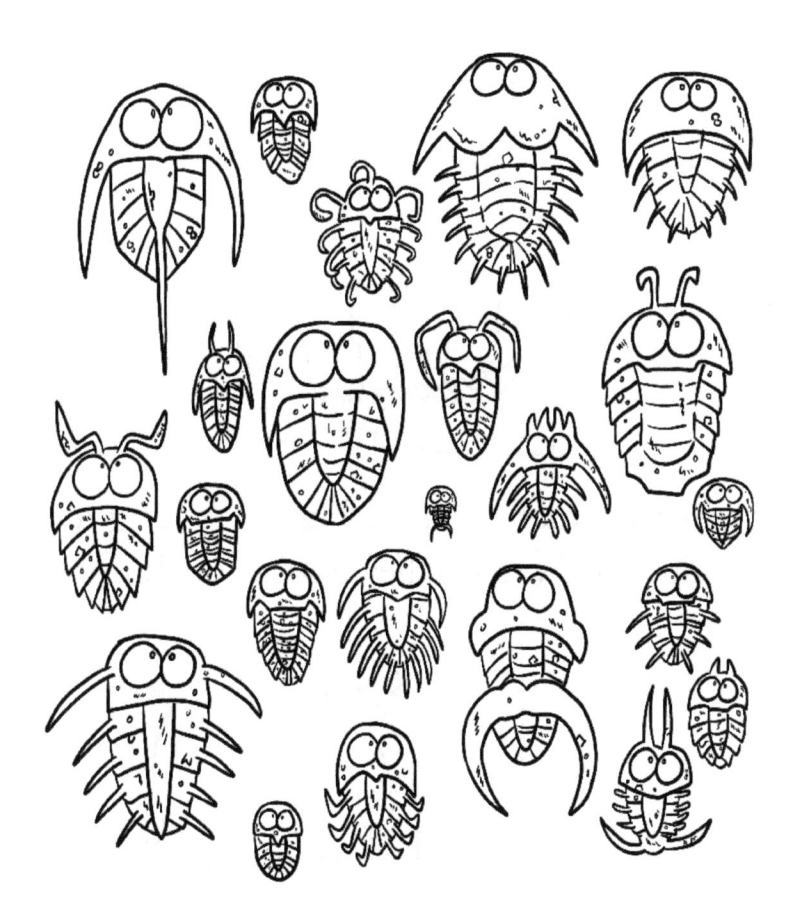

But they were all basically built like flat beetles (but with a lot more legs).

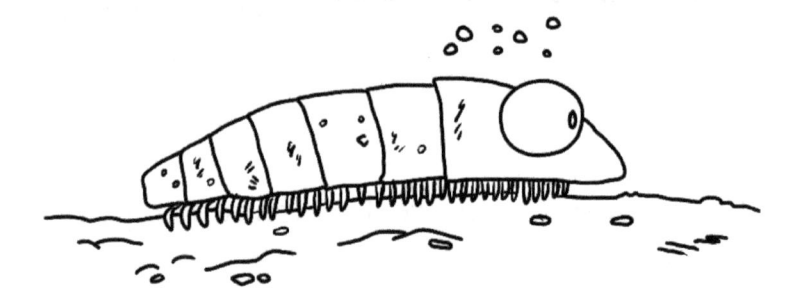

The biggest ones were 60 centimetres long (as long as two school rulers) …

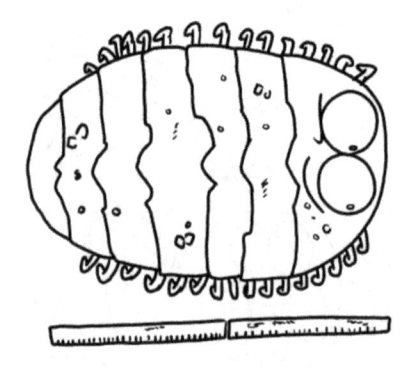

And the smallest were barely as long as a millimetre (way smaller than your thumb).

Some trilobites were hunters…

Some ate the blobs that floated around…

And some ate dead stuff they found.

Radiodonts

The radiodonts were all built like shrimp with big, weird grabber-things sticking out of their heads.

They all swam around using flaps along their sides like rows of paddles on a ship.

And they could be really, really big or really, really not-so-big.

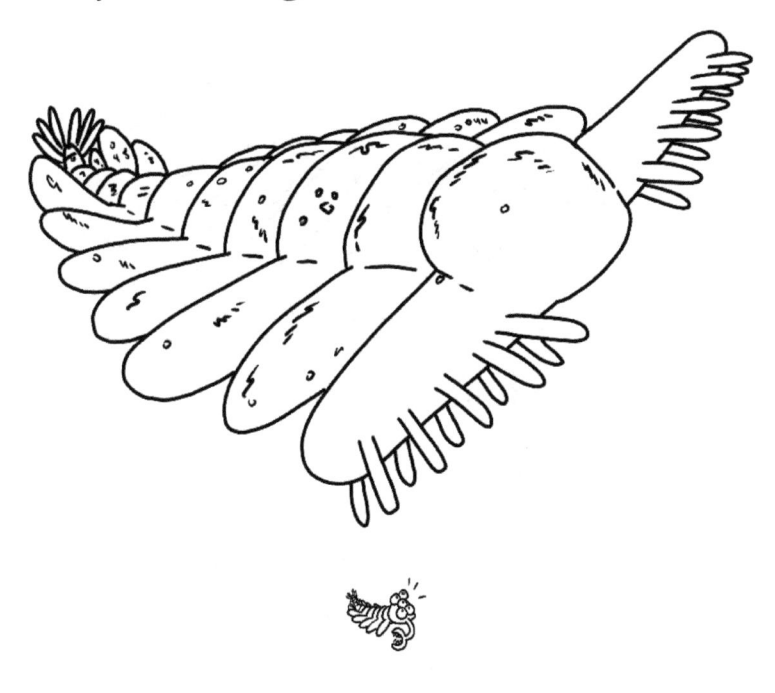

This is Opabinia. It was about 7 centimetres long (as long as a tennis ball).

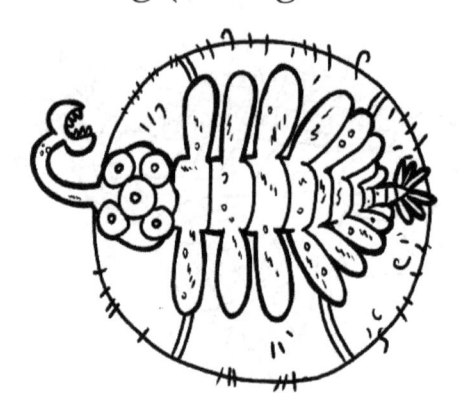

And it swam around grabbing stuff with its big arm-shaped thing…

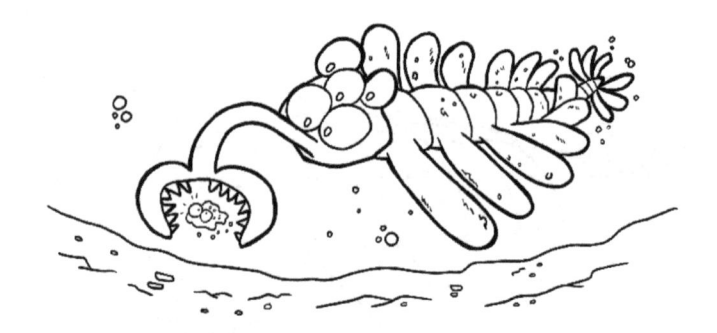

And shoving it in its mouth.

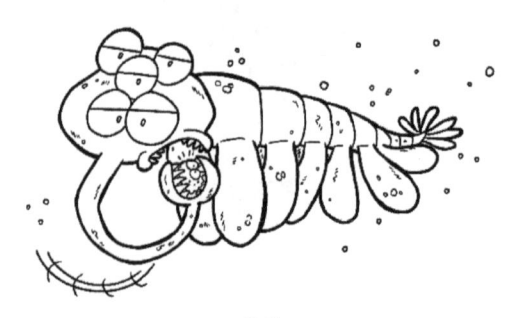

Anomalocaris was the top predator in the Cambrian. It ate everything it could grab.

And its body was about 37 centimetres long (a bit longer than a school ruler).

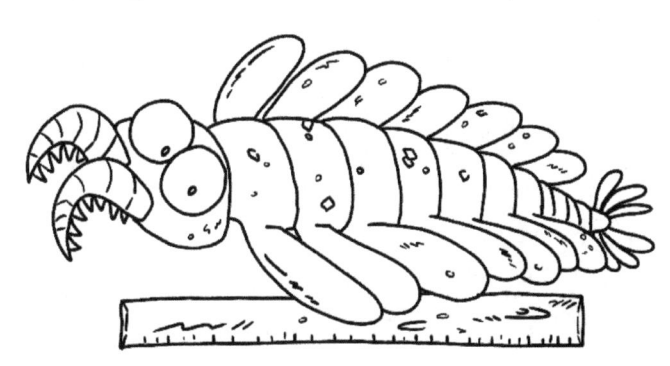

Pambdelurion was the biggest radiodont in the Cambrian.

It could grow up to 1.5 metres long (almost as tall as a regular door).

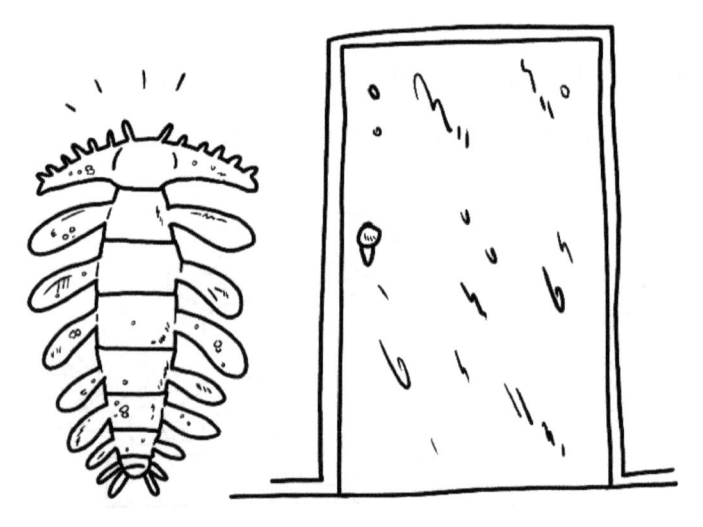

Pambdelurion had a huge set of grabber things on its head.

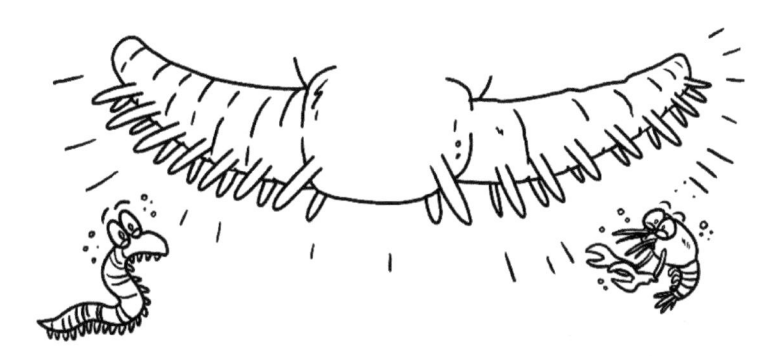

But it was probably blind (we don't even know where its eyes were) …

And it only used its grabber things to feel its way around and find blobs to eat.

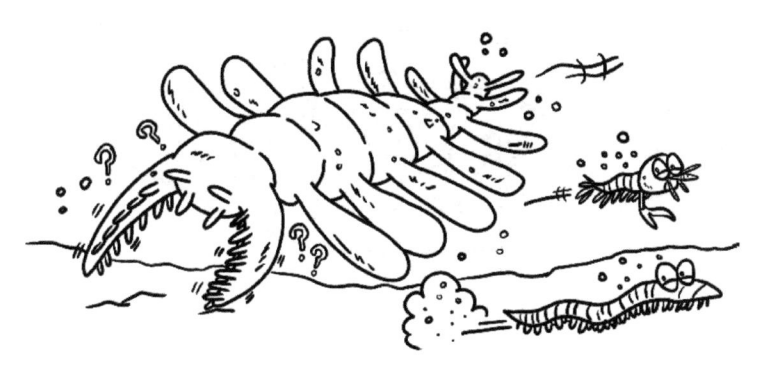

Chordates

There were a few Cambrian chordates.

They all had a bendy rod in their back which had lots of nerves out of it…

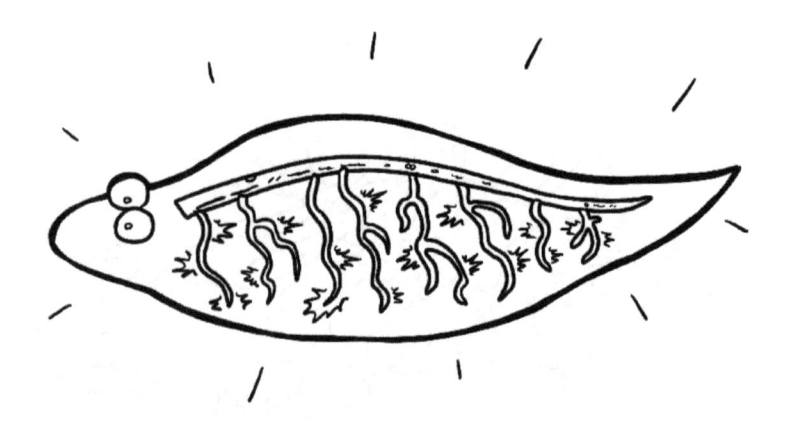

Haikouicthys is a Cambrian chordate.

It was about 2.5 centimetres long (that's not even half of a pen).

And it probably just swam around eating anything small enough to fit in its mouth.

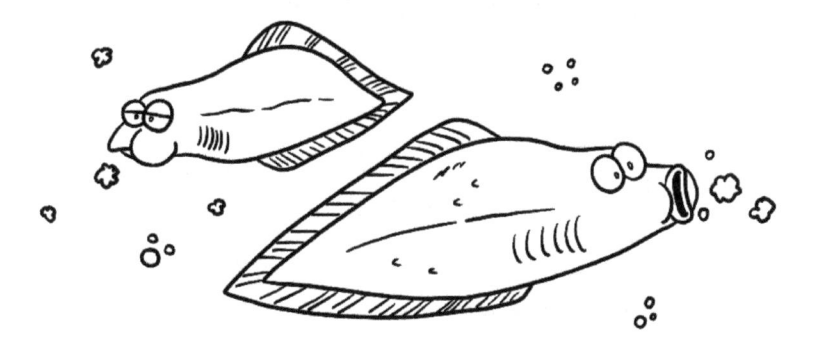

Pikaia was another Cambrian chordate.

It was about 4 centimetres long (a bit shorter than a AAA battery).

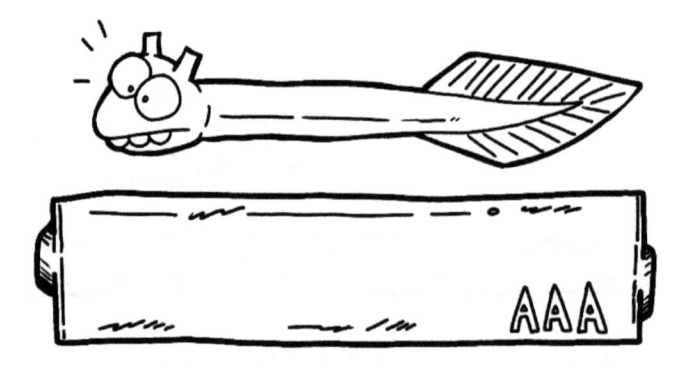

And it probably swam around eating any blobs that could fit in its mouth.

The chordates split into three types. There were the brainless blob-eating lancelets…

There were the tunicates which were either big blobs or tadpole-shaped things.

And there were the vertebrates.

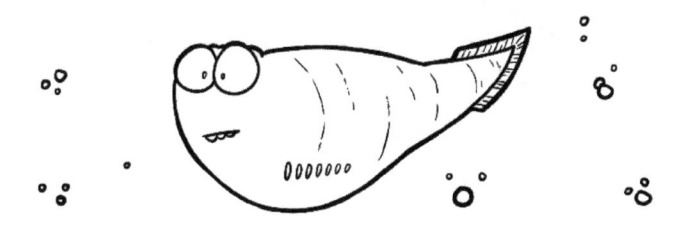

Vertebrates

Vertebrates had nerve chords like other chordates…

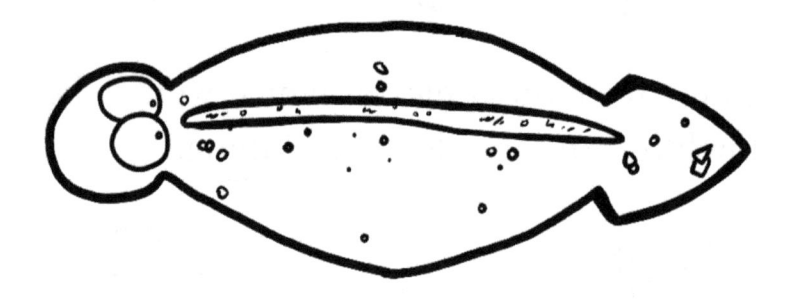

But they also evolved skeletons made of bones or this bendy stuff called cartilage.

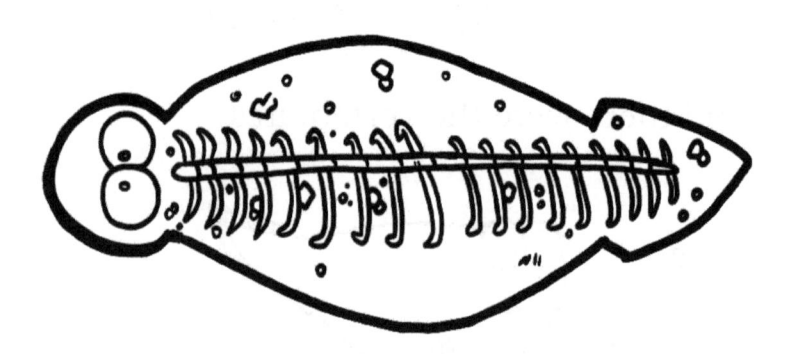

Metaspriggina was the first vertebrate we know about.

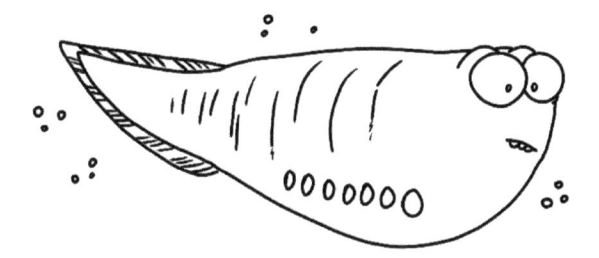

It was about 6 centimetres long (a bit longer than a AAA battery) ...

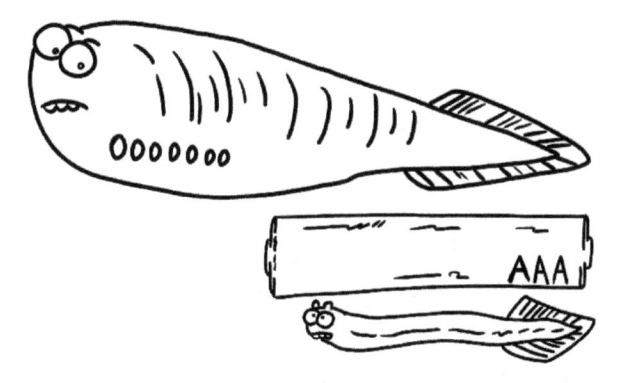

And it probably swam around near the bottom of the sea eating blobs, too.

It was also the very first fish we know about.

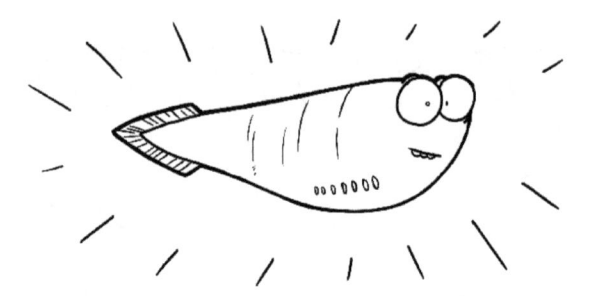

Fish are any vertebrate that breathe water using their gills…

And MOST of them have fingerless fins (Metaspriggina didn't have any, though).

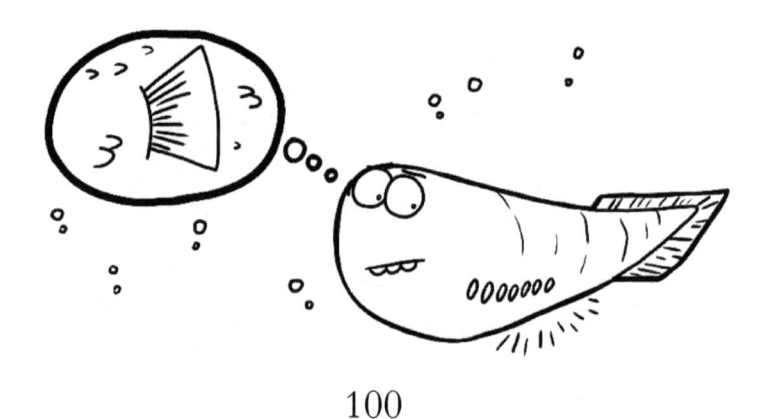

Conodonts were little vertebrates that looked a lot like eels.

They probably swam around eating stuff that floated near them.

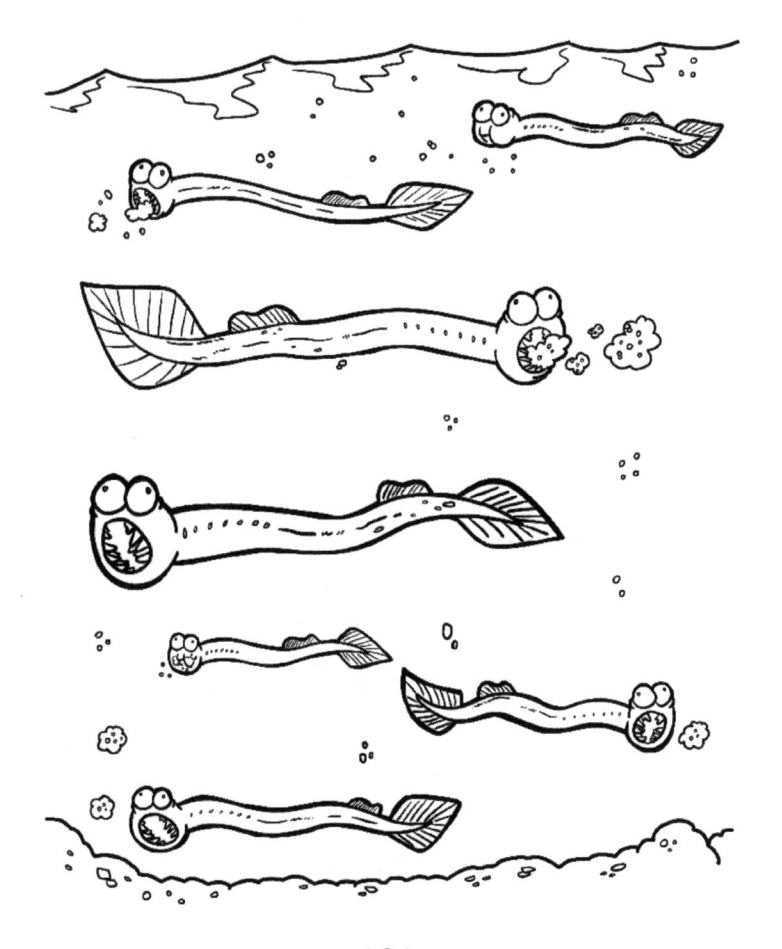

Land Plants

During the Cambrian, plants started growing on land.

They stayed where the ground was nice and soggy for them to get their water.

But there weren't any animals on land…

They were still in water…

And they weren't going to join the plants on land for millions of years.

The End of The Cambrian

Around 485 million years ago, lots and lots of animals died in a big extinction event.

Maybe the extinction was caused by sea levels going from shallow...

To being really deep…

And that can be a problem because when the ocean is shallow there's plenty of oxygen at the bottom…

But when it gets deeper, there is much less oxygen at the bottom.

Or maybe the extinction was caused by lots of volcanoes going off and pumping lots of toxic gases into the air.

No matter how it happened, the extinction event ended the Cambrian and started…

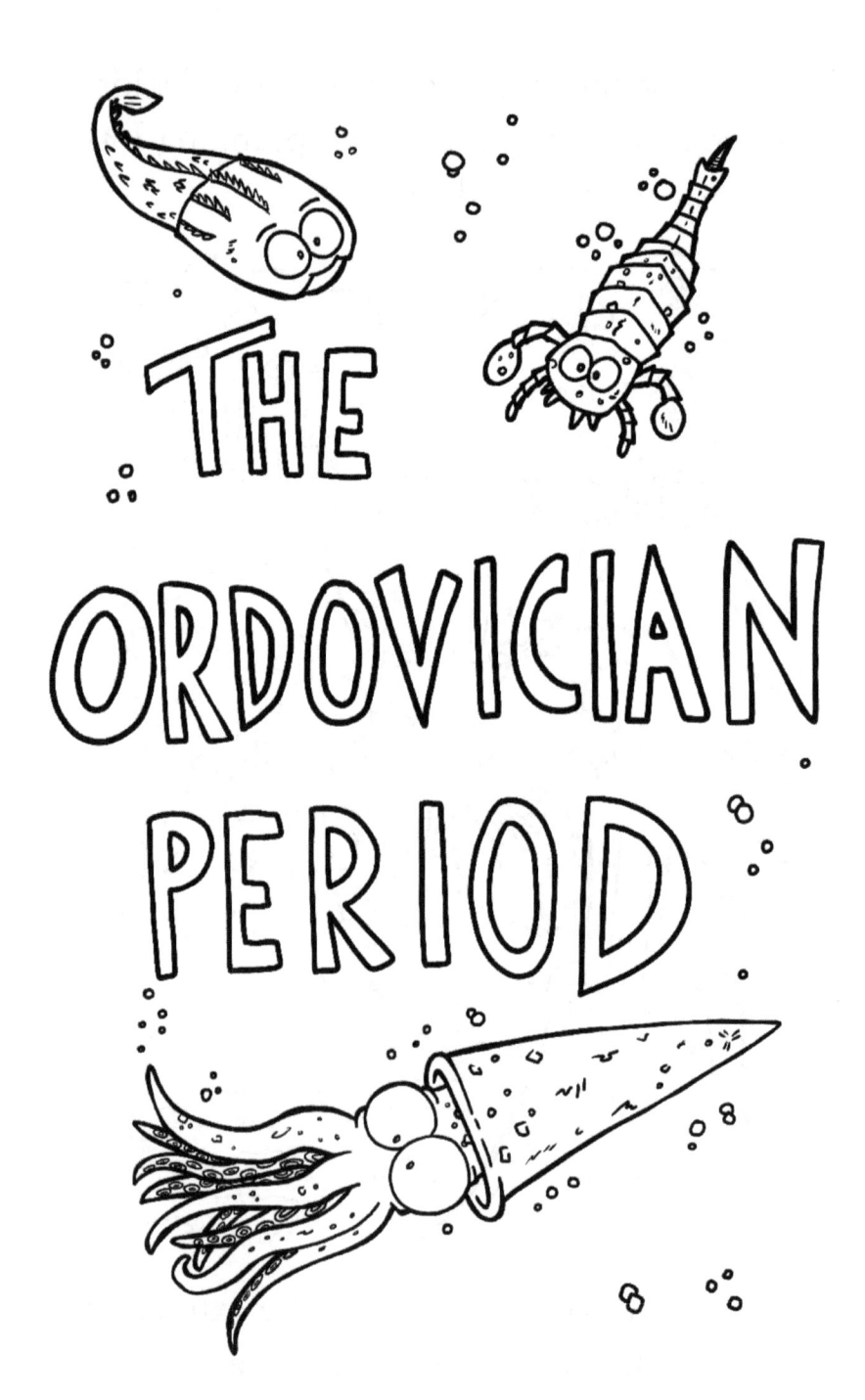

THE ORDOVICIAN PERIOD

The Ordovician period was the second period of the Paleozoic era.

It started about 485 million years ago.

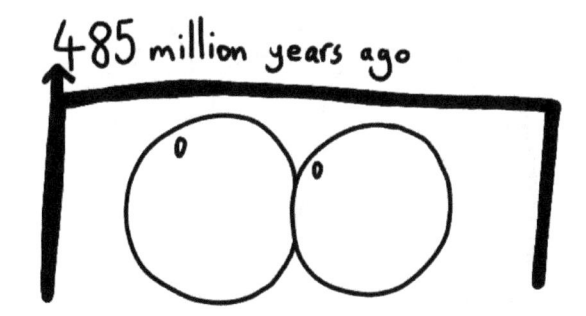

And it lasted for about 41 million years.

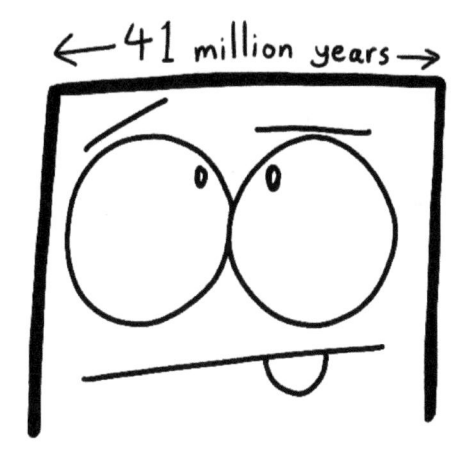

The continents were still moving north and breaking into smaller continents.

Lots of Explosions

Because of the mass extinction event at the end of the Cambrian, there were lots of gaps in the environment all over Earth.

But during the Ordovician period there were lots of explosions of new living things on Earth in lots of different places at different times.

The trilobites spread out again…

The coral started to make big reefs...

And the molluscs went all over the place.

Let's look at the molluscs up close…

Molluscs

A mollusc is any soft animal with no backbone…

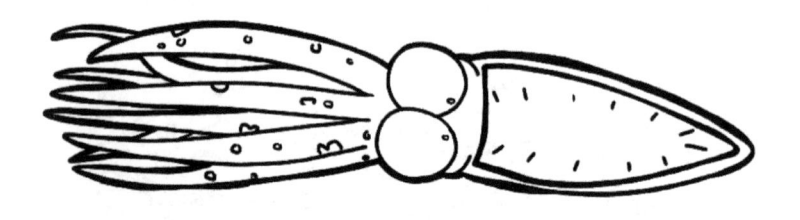

And a big flappy bit called a mantle.

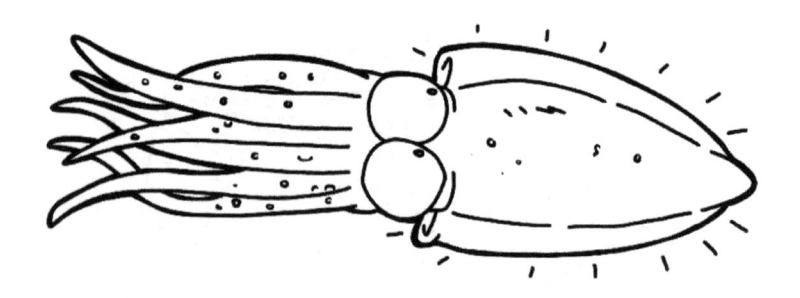

And there were three types of Molluscs: the snail-ish gastropods…

The hinge-shelled bivalves…

And the tentacled cephalopods.

In the Ordovician, the gastropods got bigger and spread out into new places…

The bivalves evolved this new stuff called byssus which let them stick to things…

And the cephalopods went from being really, really small in the Cambrian...

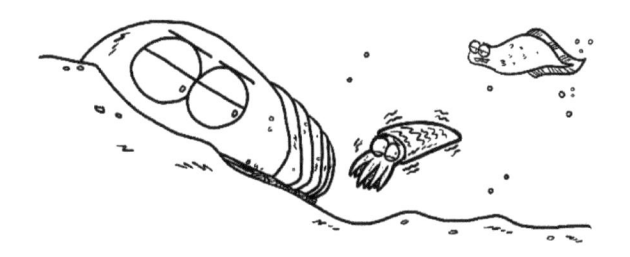

Like this tiny Plectronoceras (the earliest cephalopod we've found so far) ...

And only living in the really shallow areas of water...

To becoming some of the most dominant animals anywhere in the oceans.

Cephalopods

During the Ordovician all the cephalopods were a type called nautiloids. The nautiloid shells were usually pointy…

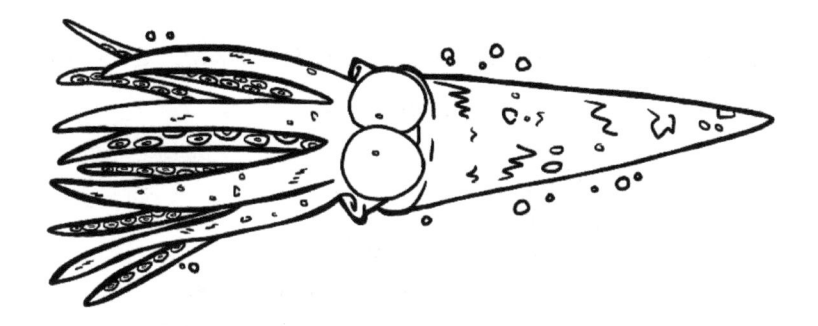

But some were also curved around.

The shells were useful because they had lots of empty pockets in them…

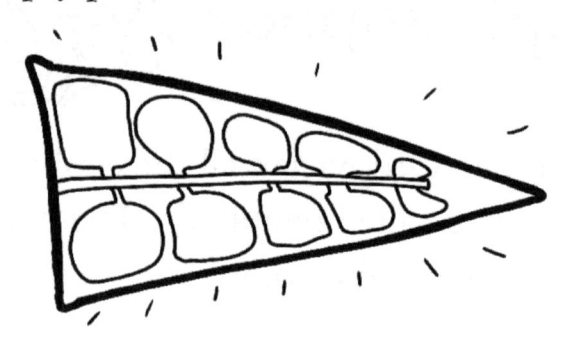

And the cephalopod could make gas go into or out of the pockets…

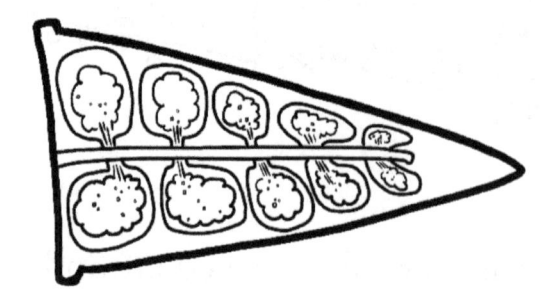

And this let it float up, sink down or stay exactly where it was in the water.

The biggest nautloid in the Ordovician period was Endoceras. It was the top predator of the Ordovician.

Its shell was almost 6 metres long (about as long as the inside of a garage).

Litoceras was one of the nautiloids with a coiled shell.

Its shell was 40 centimetres long (so a bit longer than a normal school ruler).

And it probably stayed on the ocean floor eating anything that floated by.

And because it was a bit small, other things probably tried to eat it…

But a coiled shell has a few advantages compared to a straight shell.

First, curling the shell makes it a bit stronger if something attacks…

It also makes something look bigger...

It can hide among rocks if something big and hungry comes near...

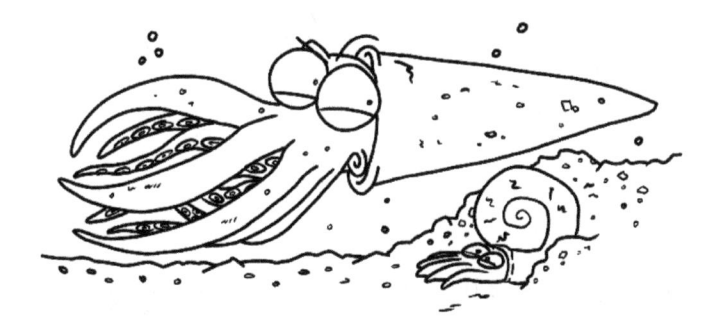

And a coiled shell is easier to steer for the nautiloid and get it out of trouble.

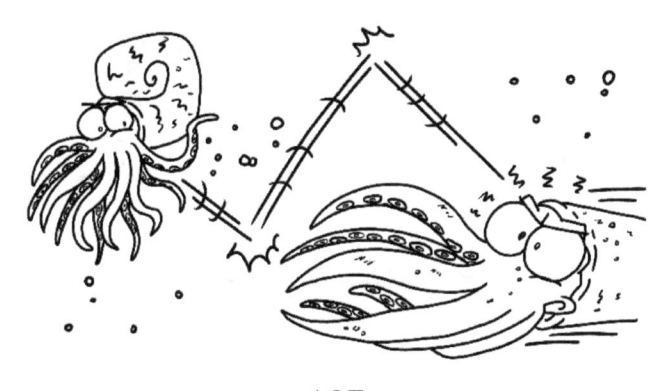

Ostracoderms

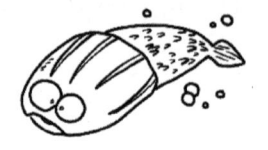

In the Ordovician there were some new fish called ostracoderms.

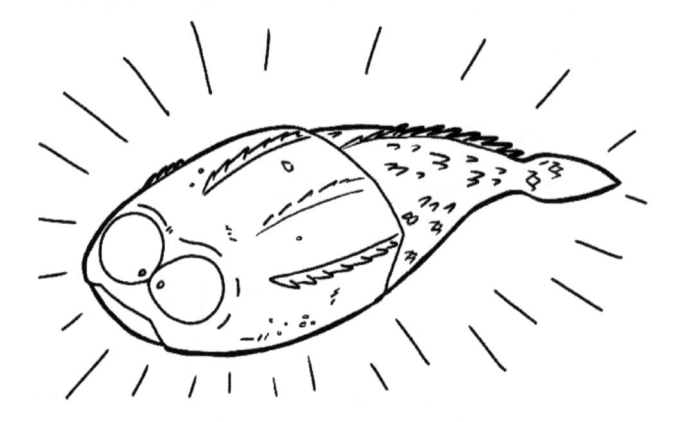

They had really hard bits covering their heads called headshields.

This is Astraspis and Sacambaspis…

Astrapsis is about 15 centimetres long (halfway along a school ruler)…

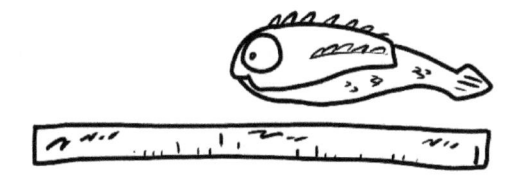

And Sacambaspis is about 30 centimetres long (the whole school ruler)…

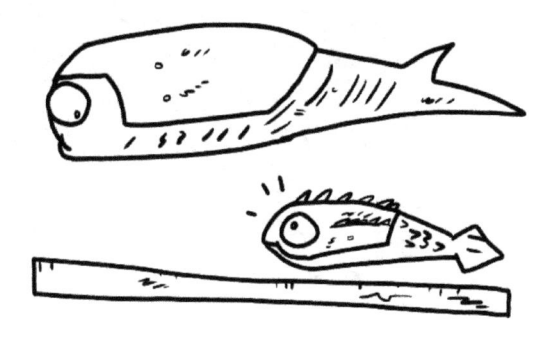

They both swam around the Ordovician near the sea floor and ate slime.

Eurypterids

Around the middle of the Ordovician, a brand-new Arthropod evolved. It was the eurypterid.

Eurypterids were pretty flat with sharp clawed-grabber bits on the front…

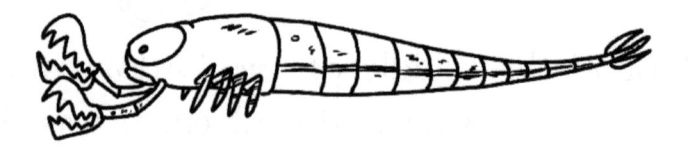

They had long tails that usually had a pointy stinger on the end…

And they could use the tails to swim.

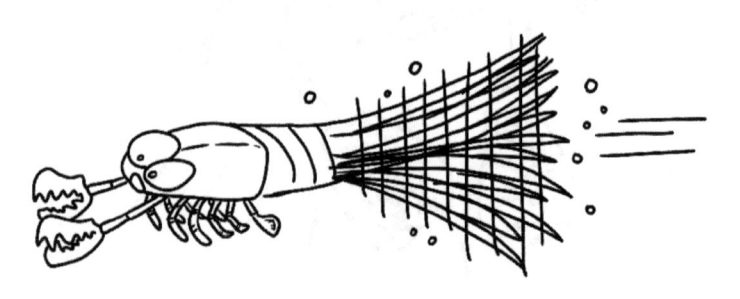

They lived in rivers and creeks with a bit of salt water in them.

And they walked along the bottom of the water looking for things to eat.

Or they'd swim around and hunt.

Most eurypterids were only about 20 centimetres (a bit over half a school ruler).

But there were also huge eurypterids like Pentecopterus.

Pentecopterus was about 170 centimetres long (almost as tall as a door).

And it went around rivers and creeks eating whatever it wanted.

Water Levels Drop

Around the end of the Ordovician, the Earth got really cold…

And there was lots of ice building up.

And all that water freezing was a problem for all the sea life.

Because when the water froze up, the water levels dropped.

And they ran out of spaces to live…

And that caused lots and lots of sea life to die off in a mass extinction event.

And that marked the end of the Ordovician period and the start of…

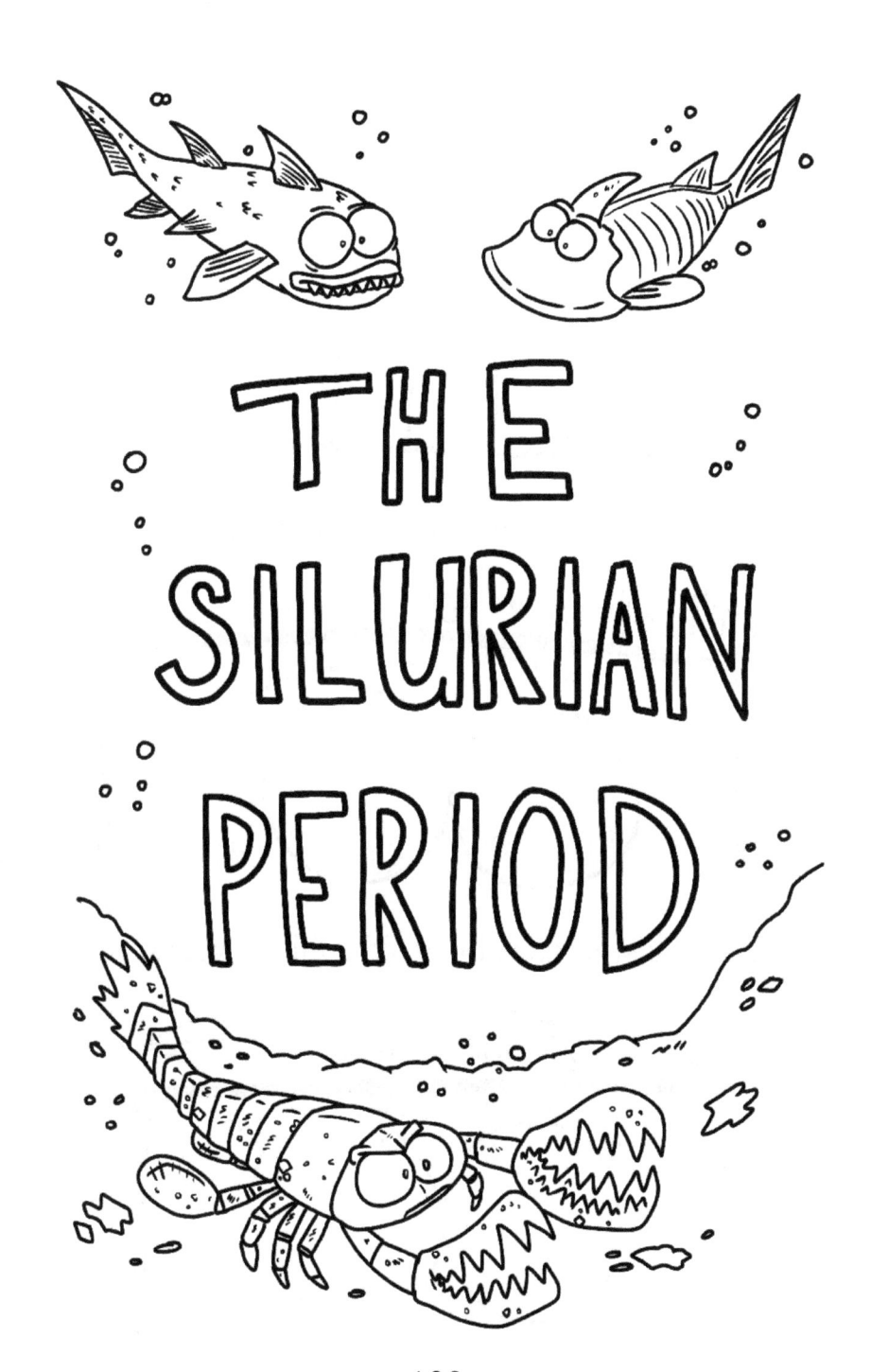

THE SILURIAN PERIOD

The Silurian period was the third period of the Paleozoic era.

It started about 444 million years ago…

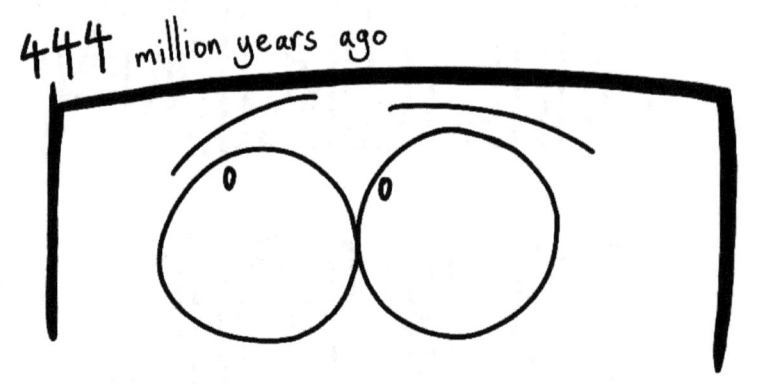

444 million years ago

And it lasted for about 25 million years.

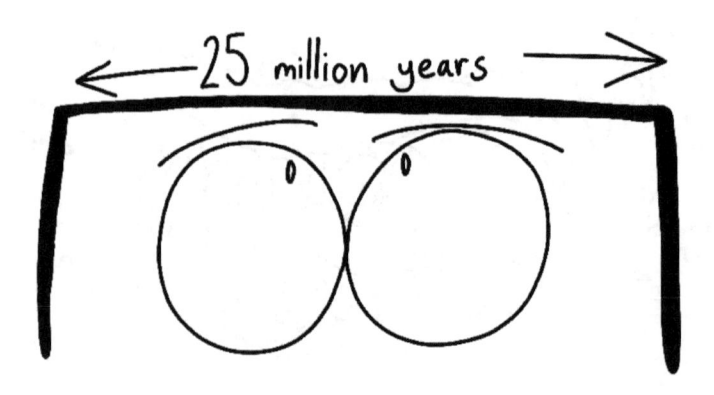

←— 25 million years —→

Most continents were in the south, but more were moving north.

Life Bounces Back

At the start of the Silurian period, Earth was still very cold and icy.

But over millions of years, it warmed up again and the ice melted away...

142

Which meant the water levels went from being a bit low…

To rising back up…

And that meant there was lots of space for life to spread out again…

But there were fewer trilobites when life bounced back…

And the nautiloids that made it to the Silurian were much smaller than before.

The eurypterids did quite well though. They became top predators.

Silurian Eurypterids

Lots of different eurypterids spread into the ponds, rivers and lakes…

They even spread out in the open oceans (which they didn't do in the Ordovician).

Some eurypterids were probably hunters.

Some were probably ambush hunters…

And some probably ate dead stuff.

Some Silurian eurypterids could probably go on dry land.

They had special gills that let them breathe in the air...

But not for long before they had to get back to the water.

Acutiramus was the biggest eurypterid in the Silurian.

Its body was about 2 metres long (that's as tall as a doorway).

And they had massive claws compared to other eurypterids.

Osteostracans

About halfway through the Silurian, a new type of ostracoderm evolved. They were called osteostracans.

Osteostracans still had big head shields, but they were really wide…

And they were probably used to sense stuff on the seafloor to suck in and eat.

They also had a pair of fins near the front and a dorsal fin near the back.

These new fins made osteostracans much better swimmers.

Which was a really good idea when you think about what they lived with.

Life On Land

About 433 million years ago this new plant evolved. It was called Cooksonia.

Cooksonia was only a few millimetres tall, but it was really, really, really important.

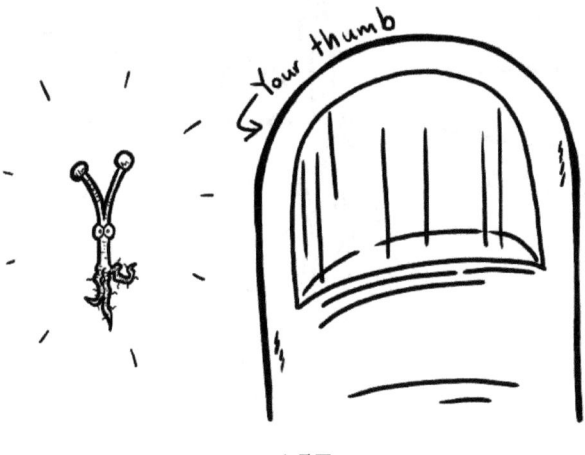

That's because Cooksonia was the first plant we know about with roots.

Roots were great because they let plants suck water up from deep underground.

That meant plants with roots could move away from waterways, spread over land…

And make Earth's very first forests.

5 million years later, animals moved onto land with the plants. They were arthropods like millipedes and arachnids.

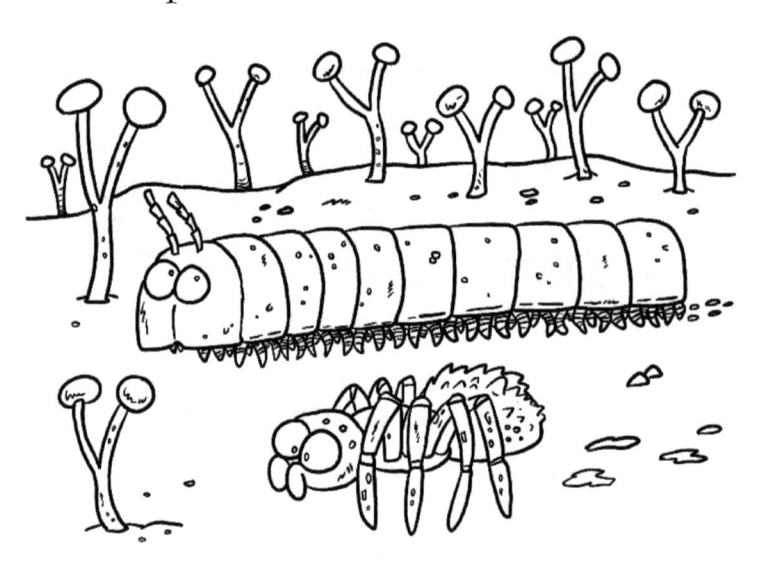

Now there are two problems for animals on land. The air could dry them out…

And the effects of gravity are much stronger in the air than in the water.

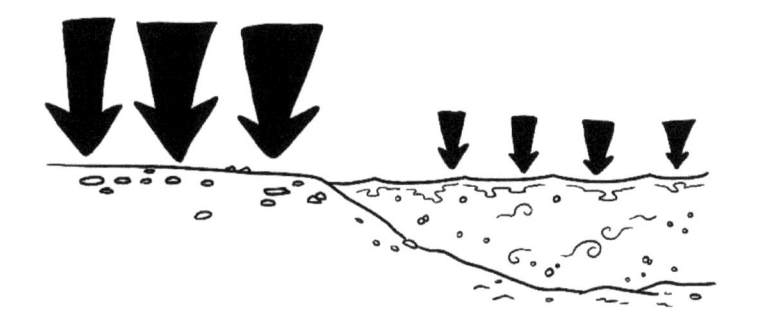

But the arthropod exoskeleton stopped them drying out…

And held their bodies up against the pull of gravity outside of water.

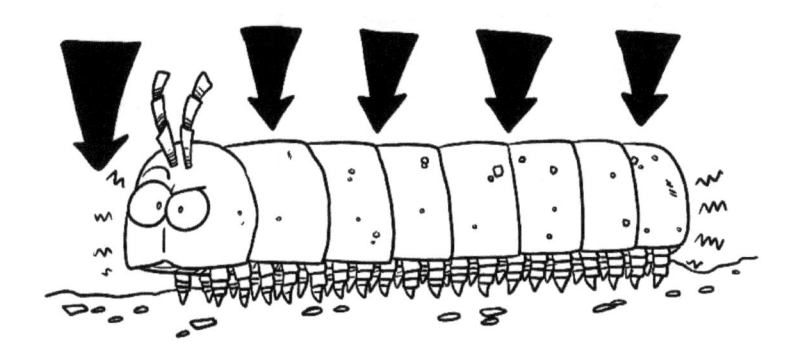

Right near the end of the Devonian these giant things called Prototaxites grew.

Prototaxites were about 8 metres tall (that's about as tall as a two-storey house). That made them the biggest living things on land so far.

Prototaxites were a fungus. Fungus live by growing off dead things (like mushrooms).

Fungus started out in the Proterozoic era as just another eukaryote.

And it started growing on land sometime during the Ediacaran period.

And by the end of the Silurian period, they were growing all over the land.

Jaws

Right near the very start of the Silurian period, this mystery fish evolved...

The only thing we know about it is that it had the very first jaws of any vertebrate.

Jaws were so great because they let fish breathe in more water much faster.

But they also helped fish grab and move stuff like rocks...

And eat things they couldn't eat before.

Around 440 million years ago, two different sorts of fish evolved from the mystery jawed fish...

They were the placoderms...

And the spiny sharks.

Placoderms

The placoderms had bony plates covering the top and bottom of their front section.

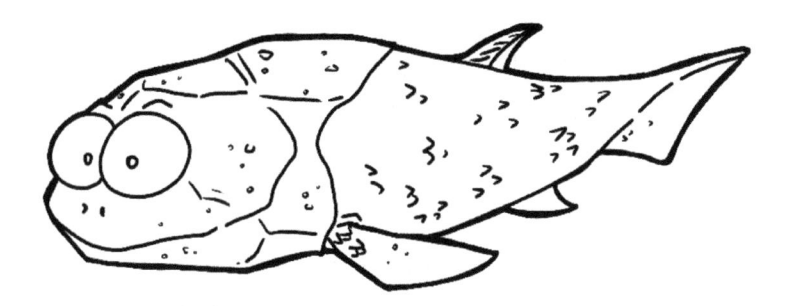

They didn't have teeth but the bony plates around their mouths acted as their teeth.

We know about three placoderms from the Silurian period. This is Silurolepis…

This is Qilinyu…

And this is Entelognathus.

All three of them probably swam around near the bottom of the sea where they could find little things to eat.

The Spiny Sharks

The spiny sharks were not really sharks but they were shark shaped.

And they were called 'spiny' because all of their fins had spines supporting them.

Most spiny sharks were only about 25 centimetres long (almost a whole ruler).

But they all came with different fins...

And different teeth (which means they ate lots of different things).

A few million years later this new type of fish evolved from the spiny sharks. They were called cartilaginous fish.

Cartilaginous Fish

Cartilaginous fish have skeletons made of cartilage instead of bone.

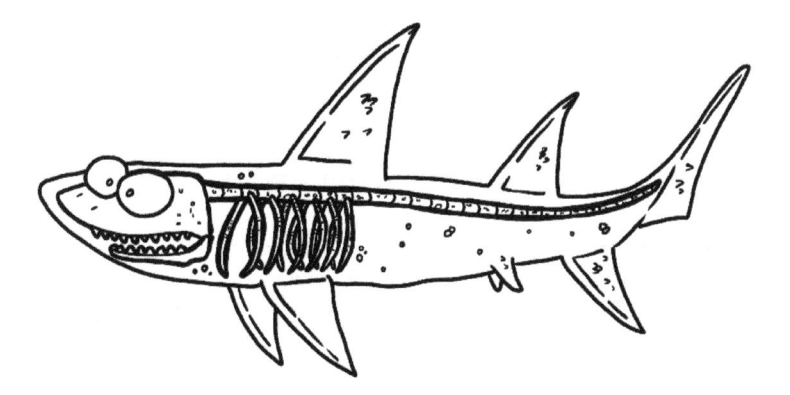

Cartilage is really bendy, and it lets the fish swim very fast.

And it makes them really flexible.

Some of the first cartilaginous fish were Qianodus and Fanjingshania.

Bony Fish

Around 418 million years ago this new fish evolved. It was called a bony fish.

Bony fish have skeletons made of hard bones (you could probably guess that).

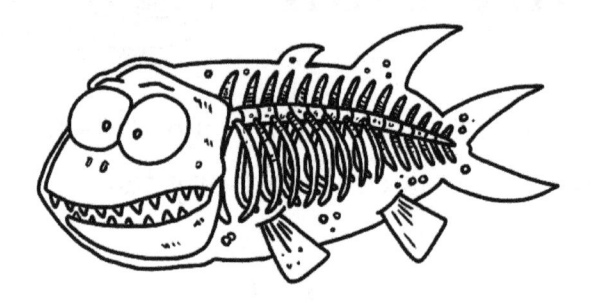

Bones are great because they keep the organs inside a fish safe from bumps.

And they support the fish's body shape.

This is Guiyu. It's one of Earth's first ever bony fish.

It was only about 30 centimetres long (that's a whole school ruler).

Guiyu had little sharp teeth which were perfect for grabbing little things.

Guiyu might have swum in open water to hunt down its prey.

Or it might have hidden and waited for things that come close enough to catch.

The End of the Silurian

About 216 million years ago, the Earth got a lot cooler…

And drier.

And the sea levels dropped really far down again…

Because of these big changes on Earth, there was another mass extinction event.

This extinction event marked the end of the Silurian period. It was time for...

THE DEVONIAN PERIOD

The Devonian period was the fourth period of the Paleozoic era.

It started about 419 million years ago.

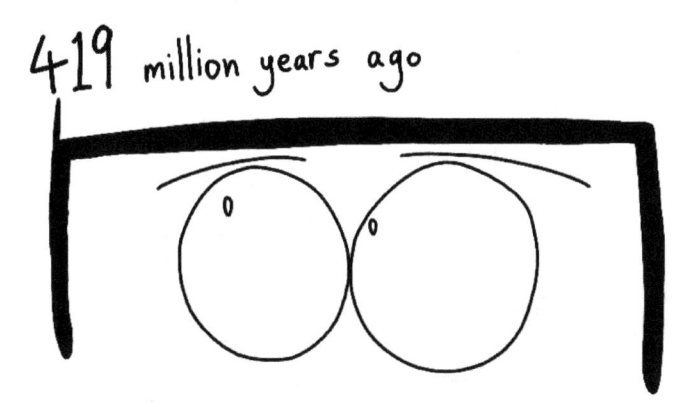

And it lasted for about 60 million years.

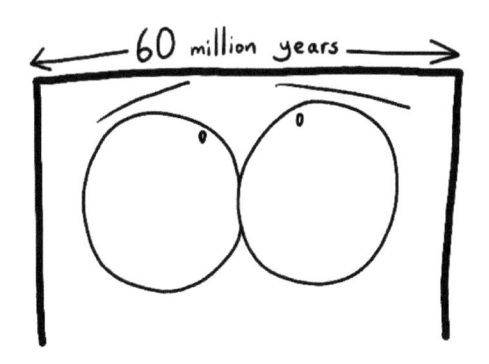

During the Devonian, the big continents kept moving further north (along with smaller continents and islands).

Eventually sea levels went up and life bounced back.

Devonian Life

Two new cephalopods evolved. They were bactritoids and the ammonoids (which mostly looked the same as the nautiloids).

But none of them were that big so lots of other things wanted to eat them.

There were lots of eurypterids in the Devonian, along with the biggest ever eurypterid- Jaekelopterus.

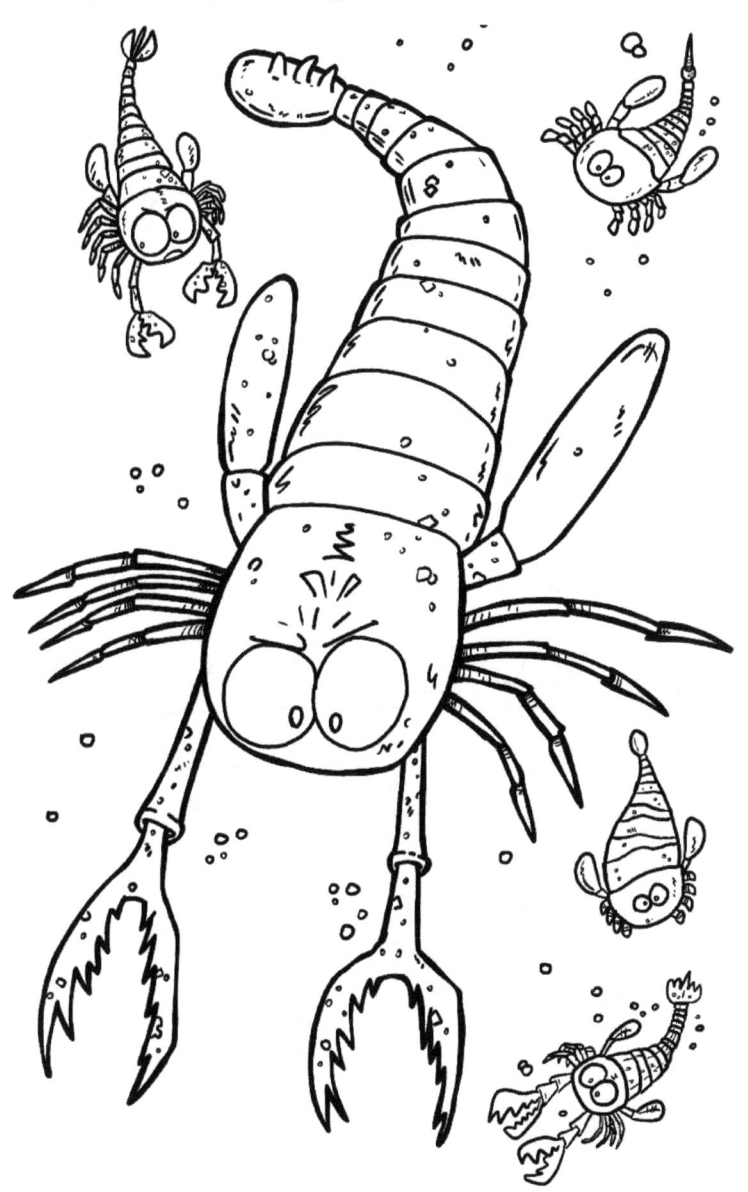

Jaekelopterus's body was about 2 and a half metres long (that's taller than a door).

It hunted around lagoons and swamps.

There were a lot less ostracoderms in the Devonian period…

But there were more and more types of placoderms evolving all over the place…

Ptyctodontida

Antiarchi

Petalichthyidae

Acanthothoraci

Rhenanida

But these are the placoderms with the biggest variety- the arthrodira!

Arthrodira

Arthrodira could move their heads more than other placoderms…

They could also open their mouths extra wide compared to other placoderms.

Rolfosteus was a really small arthrodira.

It was only 15 centimetres long.

But it had a pointy shape which let it swim around really fast.

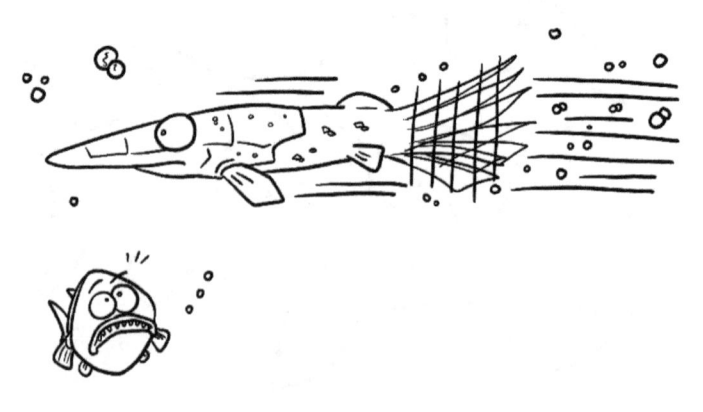

This is Phyllolepida. It was about 40 centimetres long (a bit longer than a ruler).

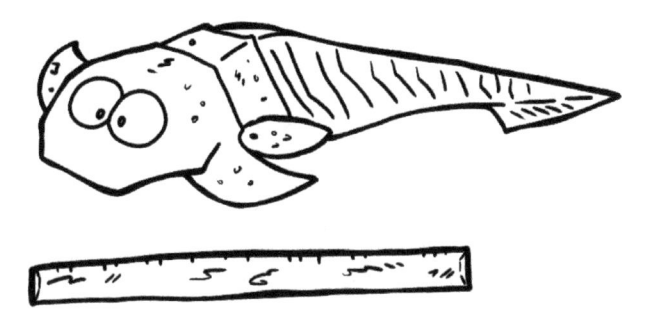

It swam around freshwater rivers and creeks...

Eating stuff it found on the bottom.

Coccosteus swam around in the open water and actively hunted smaller animals.

But because it was only about 40 centimetres long ...

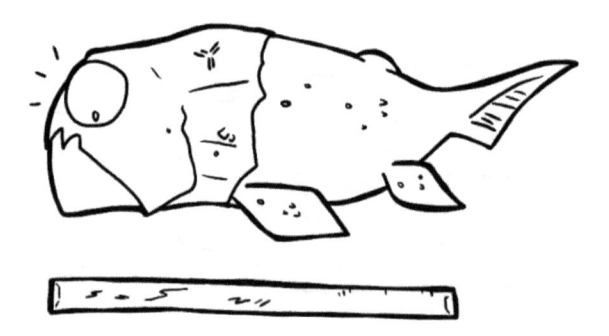

Lots of things wanted to eat it, too...

Titanichthys and Dunkleosteus were two of the biggest placoderms ever. They were both about 4 metres long (about as long as a car with a boot on the back).

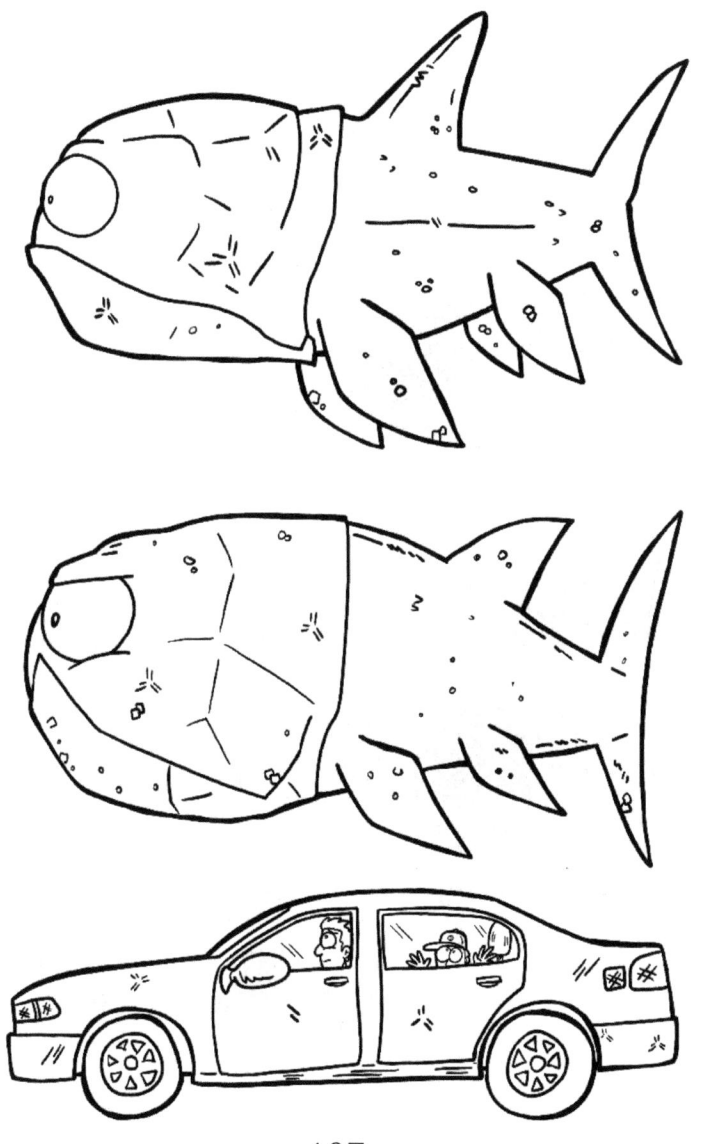

Titanichtys was big but its jaws weren't made for chomping, it probably just swam around swallowing schools of little fish.

Dunkleosteus- on the other hand- was one of the most dangerous placoderms.

It ate anything it wanted to...

Because it had very sharp, strong jaws that could snap shut very fast.

If Dunkleosteus wanted to eat something with a hard shell…

It just chewed it up…

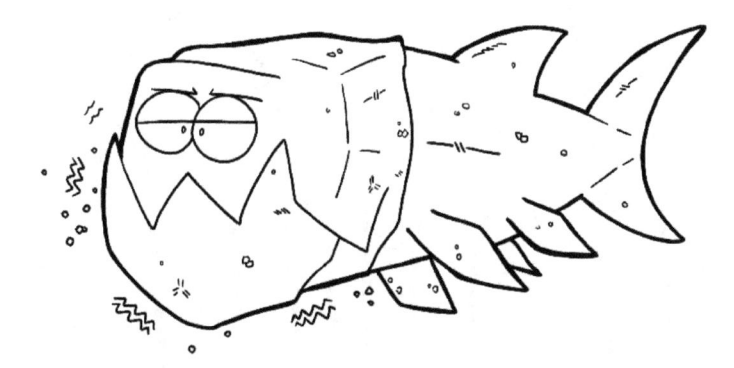

And spat out all the hard bits later.

Devonian Plants

Near the start of the Devonian, Prototaxites were still growing everywhere.

But by the middle of the Devonian, the Prototaxites were gone and there were lots of plants growing.

And by the end of the Devonian, the land was covered in big forests of woody, plants.

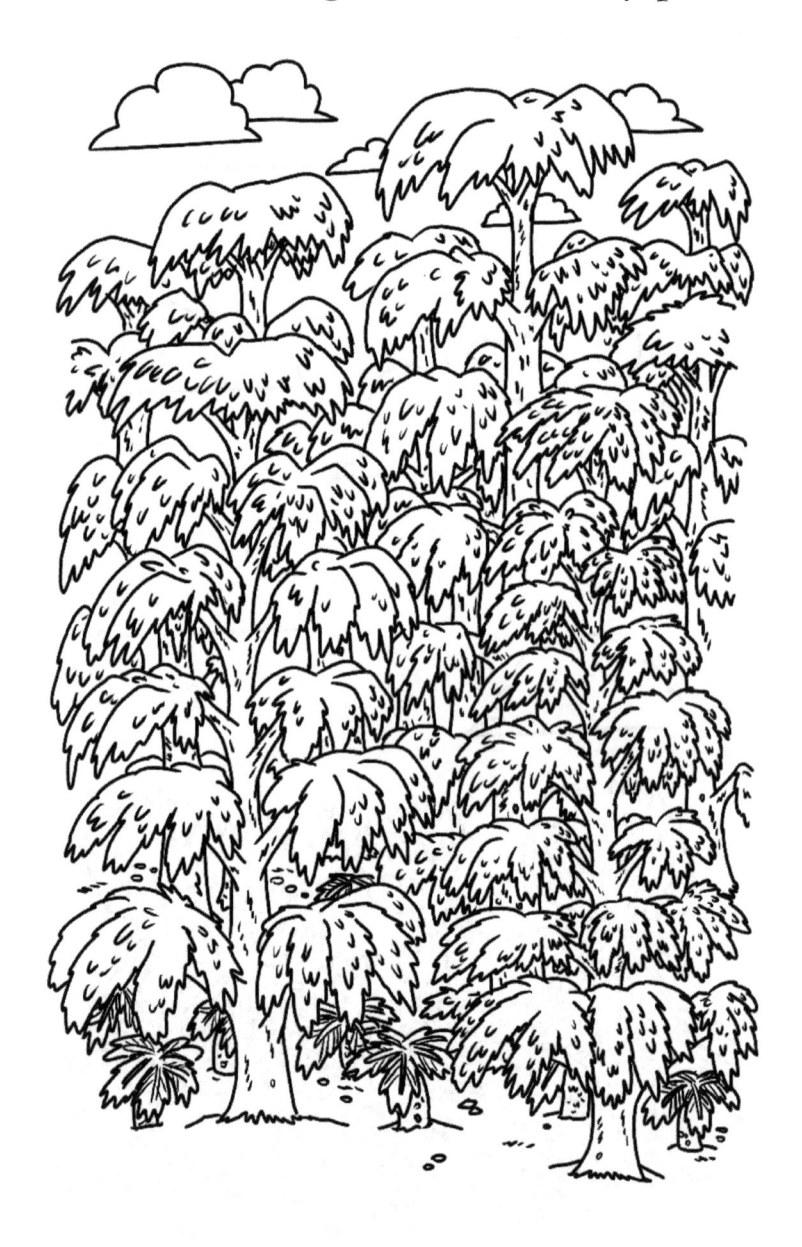

Ray-Finned Fish

Right near the start of the Devonian period a new type of bony fish evolved. They were called ray-finned fish.

Ray-finned fish have fins made of bony rays with skin stretched out between them.

Andreolepis was an early ray-finned fish that swam around in the oceans from the shallows all the way down to the deep.

Cheirolepis was another early ray-finned fish.

It was about 50 centimetres long (that's almost twice as long as a school ruler).

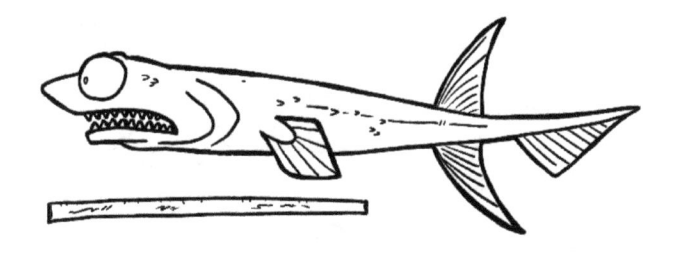

And it swam around in rivers chasing down anything small enough to eat.

Elasmobranchs

Around the middle of the Devonian period a new type of cartilaginous fish evolved. It was called an elasmobranch.

Elasmobranchs have five to seven of these lines called gill slits…

Their scales are hard and rough, like they're covered in thousands of tiny teeth.

And they have stiff fins that don't fold up.

This is Phoebodus, it's the oldest elasmobranch we know about.

It was only 1.2 metres long (that's about four school rulers put together).

But it was an ancestor to all the sharks and rays that took over oceans later.

Lobe-Finned Fish

A couple of million years after ray-finned fish evolved, another really important fish called a lobe-finned fish evolved.

Lobe-finned fish have muscles and bones in the middle of their fins.

Lobe fins are quite strong.

They help lobe-finned fish hold themselves up off rocks and the seafloor.

The lobe-finned fish are split into three big groups: these are the lungfish…

Lungfish can breathe air.

These are coelacanths. They have an extra lobe on their tail.

And these are the tetrapodomorphs.

The tetrapodomorphs had bones which were extra big and strong in their front fins.

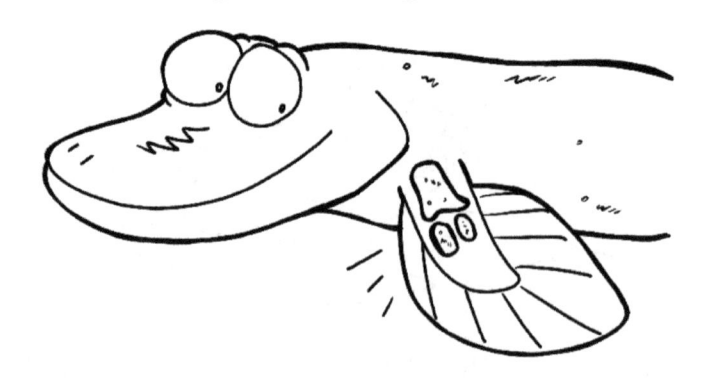

Which made the front fin even stronger.

Tetrapodomorphs

This is Tungsenia. It lived about 405 million years ago and it's the oldest tetrapodomorph we know about.

Eusthenopteron lived about 385 million years ago.

It could grow up to 2 metres long (about as tall as a door).

And even though it had really strong front fins it probably never left the water.

Pandericthys lived 380 million years ago.

And its arms were probably strong enough to hold it up on land.

And help it walk forward and back.

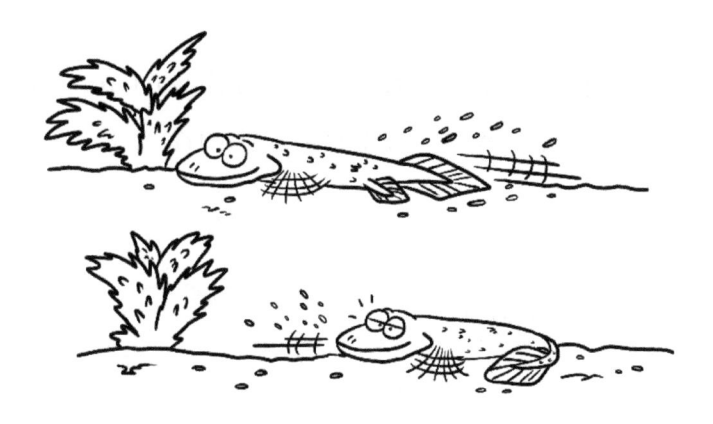

Tiktaalik lived about 375 million years ago and it had strong front limbs, too.

It was about 2 and a half metres long (a bit longer than a door).

And it may have hunted animals at the edge of the water by ambushing them.

Hyneria was a huge tetrapodomorph that lived 360 million years ago in rivers and lakes as the top predator.

And it was about 4 metres long (that's as long as a car).

Tetrapods

About 370 million years ago, this new type of tetrapodomorph evolved. They were called tetrapods.

Tetrapods were different to tetrapodomorphs because they had four strong fin legs instead of just two.

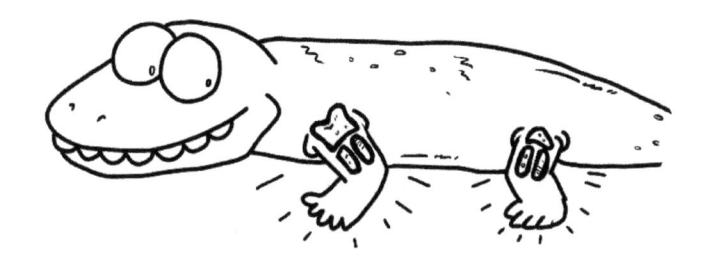

Two of the first tetrapods were Ichythostega and Acanthostega.

Ichthyostega lived 370 million years ago and it's not just a tetrapod, it's also the first amphibian we know about.

Amphibians start out as water breathers but grow into air breathers.

And they lay their eggs in water.

Ichthyostega was about 1 and half metres long (almost as tall as a door).

But even though it was big, Ichthyostega's back legs probably weren't strong enough to hold it up on land.

Acanthostega lived 365 million years ago.

It was 60 centimetres long (two school rulers put together).

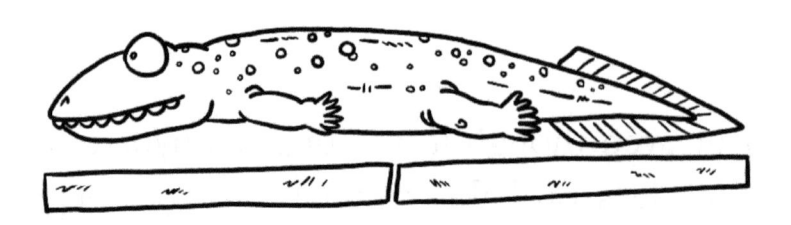

And its back legs were strong enough to hold it up (but only in shallow water).

The End Devonian Extinctions

About 382 million years ago, there was a big mass extinction event in the water...

Then about 372 million years later there was an even bigger extinction event...

And about 359 million years ago there was another one (which was not so big).

There are lots of ideas about what caused the extinctions. Maybe the volcanoes released lots of toxic gas into the air…

Maybe there was a big drop in oxygen…

Maybe the Earth got really cold…

Maybe an asteroid hit Earth...

Or maybe a supernova in space shot out a bunch of radiation which hit Earth.

We're not sure what caused them all, but we know the extinction events wiped out all the placoderms and ostracoderms.

But while things were bad in the water, life on land wasn't that badly affected at all.

The final extinction event 359 million years ago marked the end of the Devonian period and the start of...

The Carboniferous Period

The Carboniferous period was the fifth period of the Paleozoic era...

It started about 359 million years ago...

And it lasted for about 60 million years.

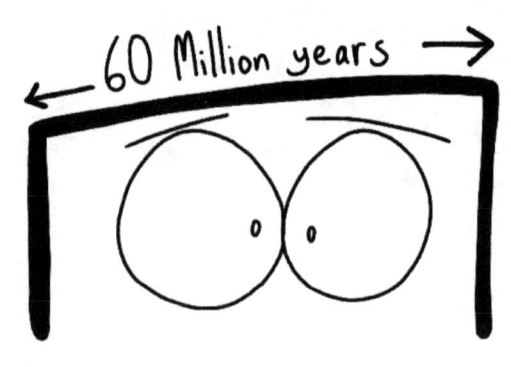

The big continents kept moving north and lots of islands were joining them.

And the Earth was really warm…

And wet.

And this led to rainforests spreading all over the land.

Life In The Oceans

With no placoderms or ostracoderms things were different in the oceans.

There were two big winners in the oceans. They were the elasmobranchs…

And the crustaceans.

The Crustaceans

Crustaceans are arthropods that usually stay in water…

And they usually have two pairs of wiggly things that look like antennae.

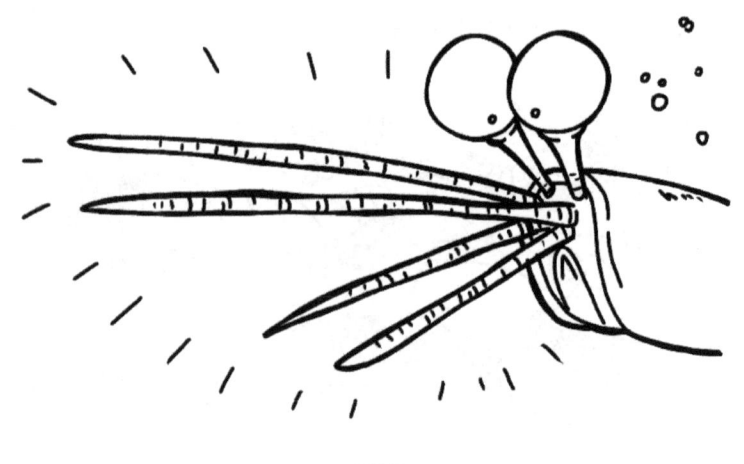

Crustaceans evolved all the way back in the Cambrian period...

But it wasn't until the Carboniferous that they spread out all over the oceans.

Elasmobranchs

With no placoderms around, the elasmobranchs took over the oceans and there were lots of different types.

Saivodus was a huge elasmobranch that ate nearly whatever it wanted to.

It could grow to about 5 metres long (a bit longer than a car) so it was one of the biggest predators in the ocean.

Stethacanthus was an elasmobranch that probably stayed near the ocean floor.

The biggest ones were about 3 metres long (almost as long as a car).

Stethacanthus had a flattened bumpy fin coming out of the top of it.

We're not too sure why it had a flat dorsal fin. Maybe the fin scared off predators…

Or maybe it helped impress other Stethacanthus during mating season.

These are the eugeneodonts.

Instead of regular teeth their jaws could have single curved rows of teeth…

Or no teeth at all…

Which they probably used to snatch little squishy fish and squid.

Edestus was the biggest eugeneodont, the biggest predator and probably the biggest Carboniferous fish in the oceans.

It was just under 7 metres long (that's almost as long as 2 cars).

And it probably used its two rows of teeth to grab and slice through anything it could catch up to in the oceans.

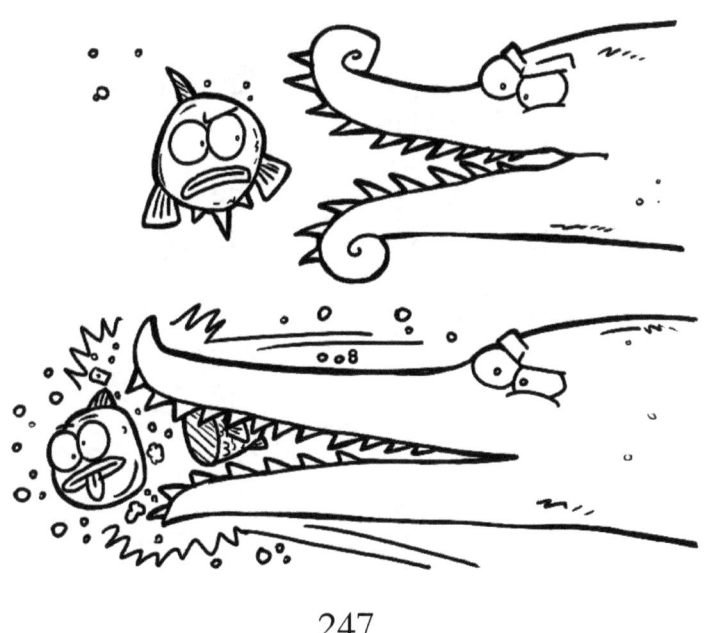

These are the Iniopterygiformes.

Yes, I know the name is complicated.

Try to say it slowly.

In-Ee-O-Terry-Gi-Forms.

Nice one. You've got it.

They only grew up to about 50 centimetres (that's 1 and a half school rulers long).

But they had big fins on each side.

The wings probably helped them swim really fast when a predator got too close.

And maybe they even helped Iniopterygiformes come out of the water and flap away in the air for a little while.

Life In Rivers And Lakes

In the rivers and lakes there were lots of crustaceans and even a few eurypterids…

251

There were also the usual lungfish, spiny sharks, bony fish…

There were also elasmobranchs in the rivers and lakes. This is Bandringa.

It was about 50 centimetres long (almost two school rulers).

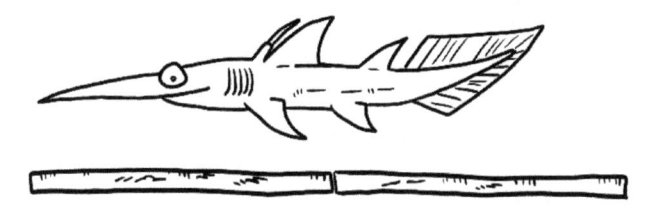

They went around and sucked up things they sensed things with their rostrum (that's the long bit at the front).

Xenacanthids were big elasmobranchs that went around as nearly the top predators.

They grew to about 5 metres long (a bit longer than a regular car).

But the scariest freshwater fish at the time were a group of lobe-finned fish called the rhizodonts.

The rhizodonts had big strong jaws and really sharp teeth.

They would hunt by grabbing other fish that got too close…

And shaking them to pieces.

The biggest rhizodont (and the biggest freshwater fish ever) was Rhizodus.

Rhizodus was about 7 metres long (that's almost two cars long).

And it ambushed and ate anything that got too close.

The Amphibians

During the Carboniferous period, the amphibians spread out in water and land.

Amphibamus was only about 15 centimetres long (half of a school ruler).

It had strong legs for running…

And a big flat tail for swimming.

The amphibian Ophiderpeton looked a lot like a snake.

It was only 15 centimetres long (that's half a ruler long).

And it probably went around hunting down little bugs.

This is Dendrerpeton. It was about 35 centimetres long (a bit longer than a ruler).

It probably went around eating lots of little insects, too…

But it could also eat other small amphibians.

Diplocaulus was about a metre long (halfway up a normal door).

And it would have been a predator in the rivers that it swam around…

Crassigyrinus and Anthracosaurus were two of the biggest amphibian predators in the Carboniferous.

They were both about 3 metres long (almost as long as a car).

Crassigyrinus probably swam through the rivers hunting down fish.

And Anthracosaurus probably hunted on the land and shallow water.

The Amniotes

Near the start of the Carboniferous period, new Tetrapods evolved called amniotes.

There are lots of differences between amphibians and amniotes.

But one of the biggest differences is the tough amniote egg.

The amniotes eggs were so tough they didn't dry out when laid outside of water...

This meant the amniotes didn't have to live near water like the amphibians…

And that meant they could spread out into all the areas that amphibians couldn't get to.

Casineria is one of the first amniotes. It evolved about 340 million years ago.

It was only about 15 centimetres long (half of a school ruler).

And it was one of the first animals with claws.

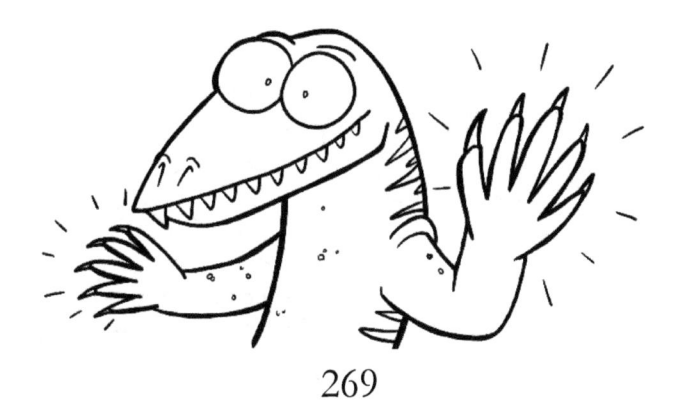

Then, about 320 million years ago, two groups of amniotes evolved- the sauropsids and synapsids. They looked very similar…

But the big difference between them was their skulls.

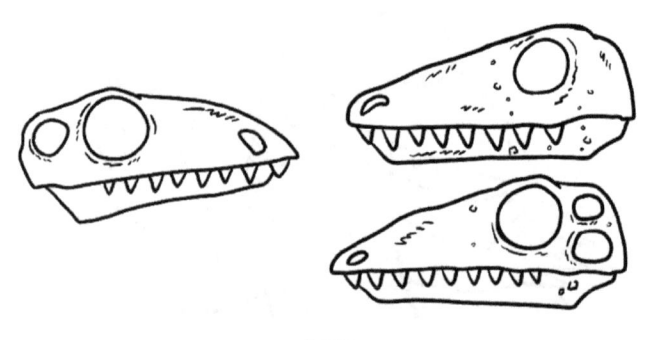

Sauropsid skulls have can have no extra holes in their skulls…

Or they have two extra holes on each side behind their eyes.

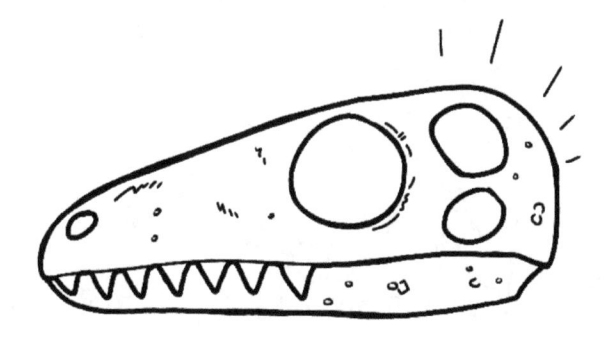

And synapsid skulls have one extra opening on each side of their skull.

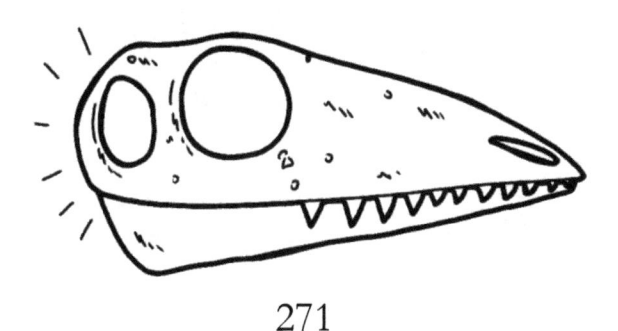

The Sauropsids

In the Carboniferous all the sauropsids were small and lizard-shaped.

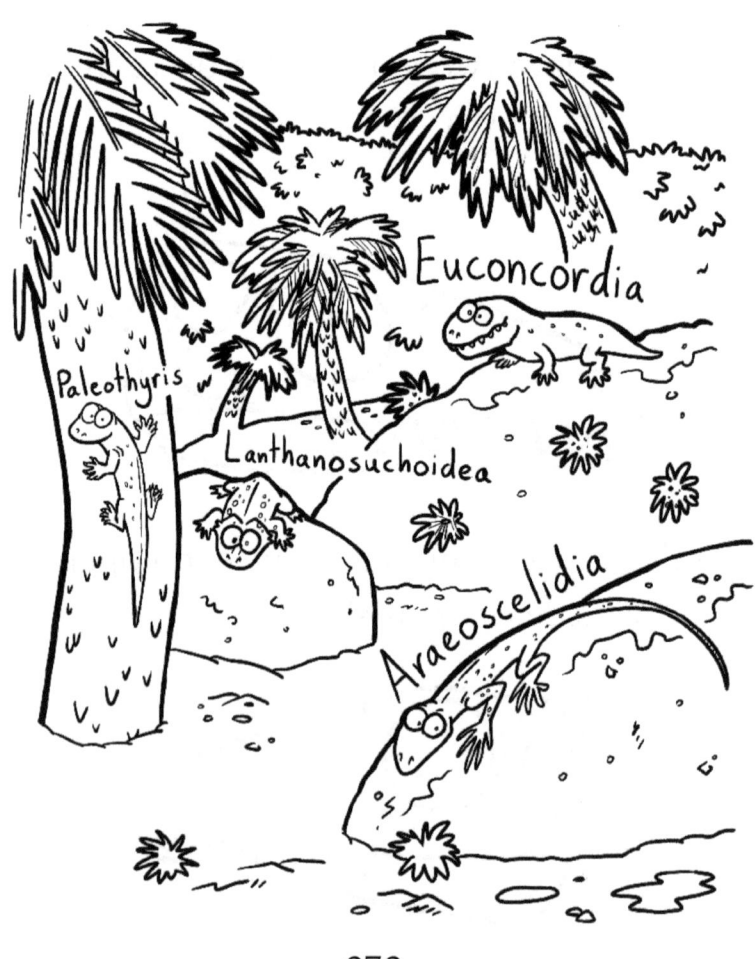

Hylonomus was the earliest Sauropsid we know about. It lived 312 million years ago.

It was about 20 centimetres long (that's almost as long as a school ruler).

And it probably ran around eating insects and other little bugs it could catch...

The Synapsids

Echinerpeton and Archaeothyris were the first synapsids. They evolved about 306 and 308 million years ago.

Ophiacodon was one of the biggest synapsids in the Carboniferous.

It was 3 metres long (almost as long as a car).

The sail-back synapsid Macromerion was a hunter, too.

But it was a bit smaller at about 1.5 metres long (almost half a car).

The Edaphosaurs were a group of sail-backed synapsids that ate plants.

They were also the very first herbivorous amniotes we know about.

The sails on their backs could have been for catching heat from the Sun.

Or they could have been for attracting sail-backs they liked.

Or they could have been for scaring off sail-backs they didn't like.

The Land Arthropods

The Carboniferous arthropods that lived on land got really, really big.

Arthropleura was the biggest arthropod to live on land ever. It probably went around on the forest floor eating seed and leaves.

And it was about 2.5 metres long (that's almost as long as a car).

Pulmonoscorpius was the biggest scorpion ever. It probably hunted around the forest floor eating anything small enough to catch.

It was about 70 centimetres long (that's two school rulers plus a little more).

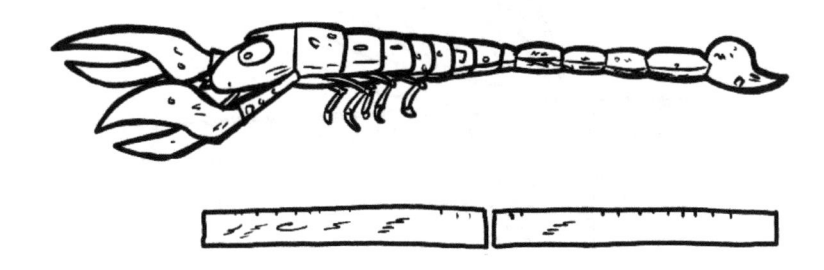

Meganeura was the biggest flying arthropod ever. It probably flew through the air snatching things with its front legs.

And it was about 40 centimetres long (that's one school ruler plus a bit more).

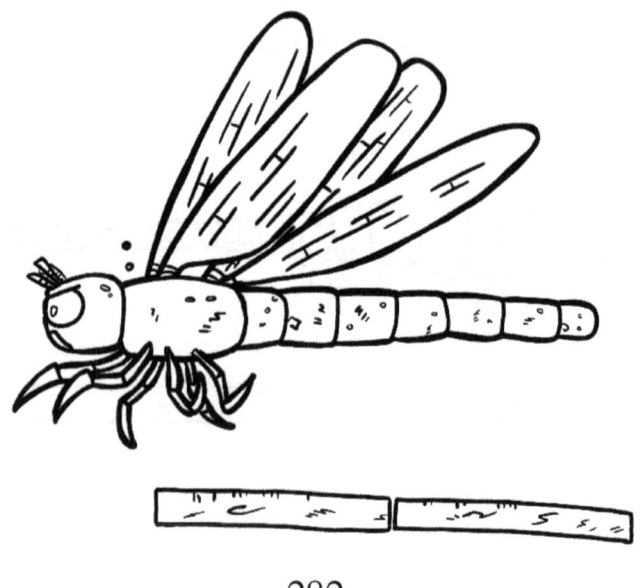

The Rainforest Collapse

Earth started really cooling down around 305 million years ago. It got so cold that there were glaciers forming in the south.

And because the glaciers formed, the water levels dropped again…

Not only that, but there was also less rain spreading out over all the rainforests.

And that caused lots of rainforests to dry up…

And be replaced with big dry spaces.

The amphibians lost a lot of places to live.

The big arthropods went extinct…

And so did the big scary rhizodonts.

The rainforest collapse marked the end of the Carboniferous period and the start of…

THE PERMIAN PERIOD

The Permian period was the sixth period of the Paleozoic era.

It started about 299 million years ago.

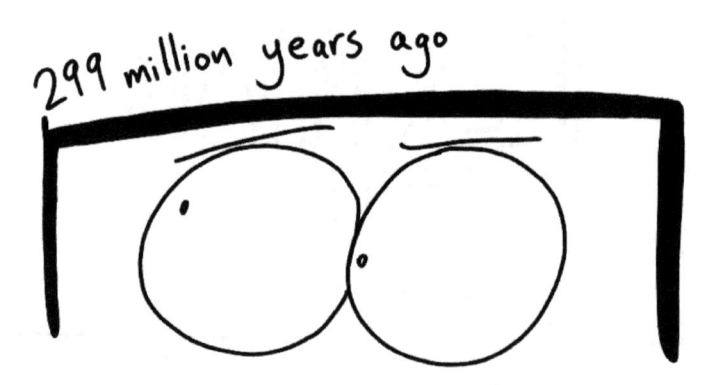

And it lasted for about 47 million years.

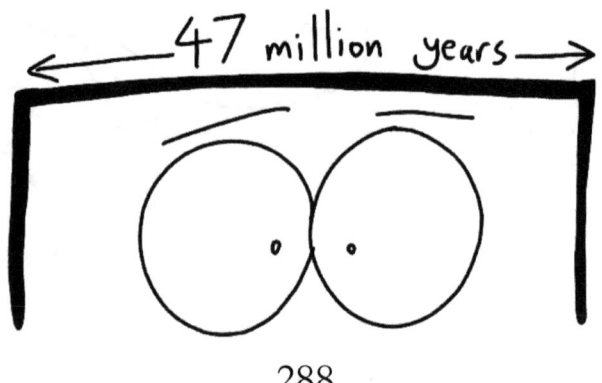

At the start of the Permian, most of the continents had grouped together to make one big continent.

In The Oceans

In the sea of the Permian period, life was pretty close to how it was in the Carboniferous period.

Around the beginning of the Permian period, the top predator in the seas was the eugeneodont Helicoprion.

It was about 11 metres long (that's over two cars long).

And it probably used its big tooth wheel to catch soft and hard-shelled animals.

Then around the middle of the Permian, there were lots and lots of these elasmobranchs called hybodonts.

Hybodonts were a type of elasmobranch with spikes on their top fins.

Rivers And Lakes

During the Permian period, the freshwater environments had changed a little…

There were lots of arthropods like dragonfly larva, water mites and even a few eurypterids…

There were lots of lungfish...

And hybodonts…

And because the rhizodonts went extinct, the xenacanthids became top predators.

The Amphibians

The amphibians lost a lot of habitats when the rainforests collapsed but there were still lots of them around near the waterways…

Plathystrix was a sail-backed amphibian that probably had to avoid being eaten by a lot of much bigger amphibians.

It was only about 1 metre long (halfway up a door).

Eryops was one of the biggest animals on land at the time. It hunted along the edges of waterways.

It grew to about 2 metres long (that's about half the length of a car).

Proterogyrinus was a predatory amphibian that hunted animals on the edge of rivers…

It was about 2 and a half metres long (over half of a car).

Gaiasaia had big fangs on its bottom jaw, and it spent its time hunting in the water.

It probably grew up to 4 metres long (as long as a car).

And Prionosuchus was the biggest amphibian ever.

It was about nine metres long (that's nearly two and half cars long).

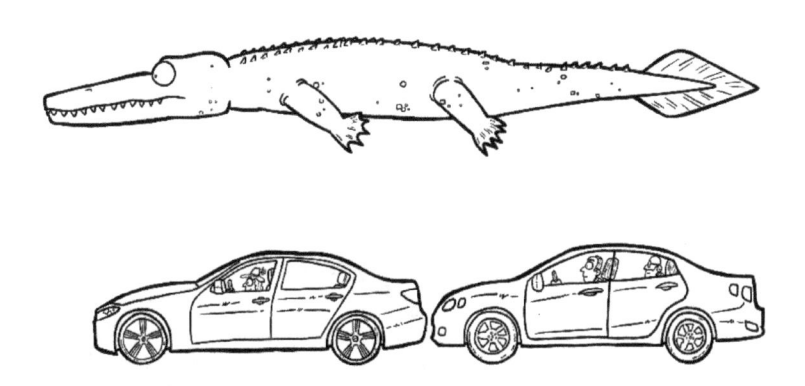

And it was one of the top predators in the rivers and lakes.

Sauropsid Skulls

Remember when I said that the sauropsids had two extra openings in their skulls...

Or none at all?

Well, the sauropsid with two extra openings in their skulls are called...

DIAPSIDS

And the sauropsids with no extra openings in their skulls are called…

ANAPSIDS

The sauropsids spread out into two big groups: the parareptiles and the eureptiles.

The parareptiles USUALLY had anapsid skulls…

And the eureptiles USUALLY had diapsid skulls.

The Parareptiles

Lots of parareptiles were lizard shaped. They spent their time running around hunting insects in the Permian…

Mesosaur was the first parareptile (and the first sauropsid) to go back to life in the sea.

And it was about a metre long (that's halfway up a door).

Eudibamus was the very first parareptile and sauropsid that could walk on two legs.

It was about 26 centimetres long (almost as long as a school ruler).

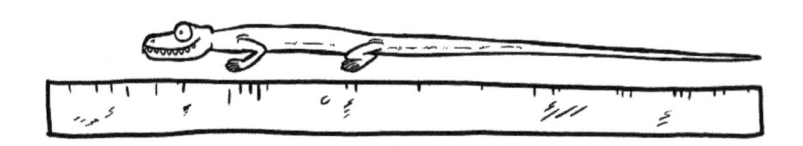

And because of the way it moved on two legs, it was probably really, really fast.

Coelurosauravus was the very first land vertebrate that could glide.

It was about 35 centimetres long (a bit longer than a school ruler) and its wings were each 30 centimetres long.

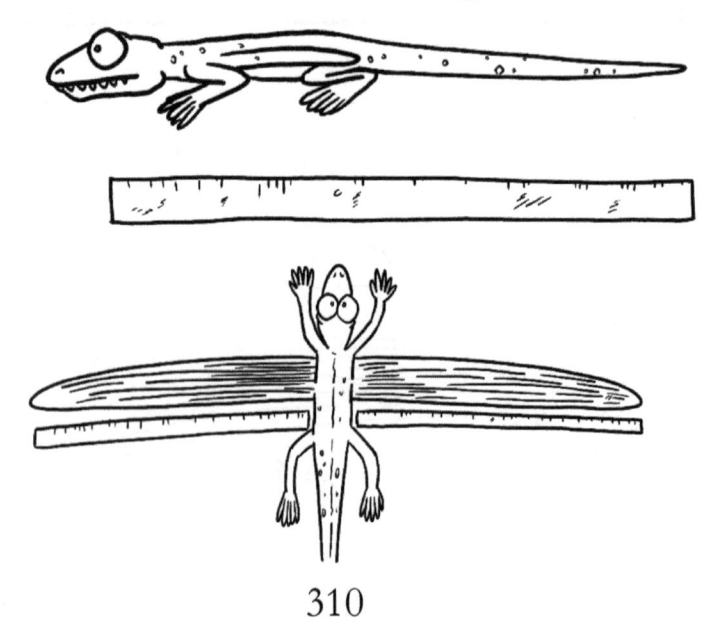

Eunotosaurus had a wide back and its rib bones worked together like a turtle shell.

Its body was about 30 centimetres long (a whole school ruler).

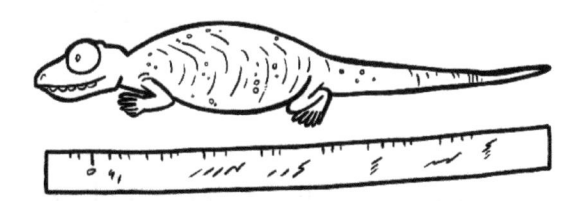

The big rib cage worked as a shell when bigger things tried to eat Eunotosaurus.

But Eunotosaurus was a bit of a mystery...

Eunotosaurus grownups had anapsid skulls like other parareptiles...

But Eunotosaurus baby skulls had ONE extra hole! So, were they anapsids or not?!?!

There were also these big parareptiles with thick bony back plates called Pareiasaurs.

Pareiasaurs ate ground plants (which made them the first plant-eating sauropsids).

The biggest Pareiasaurs were about three metres long (almost as long as a car). This made them the biggest Permian sauropsid.

And by the end of the Permian period, they'd spread all over Earth.

The Eureptiles

In the Permian, all the eureptiles looked a lot like lizards. There were lots of lizard-shaped eureptiles on land…

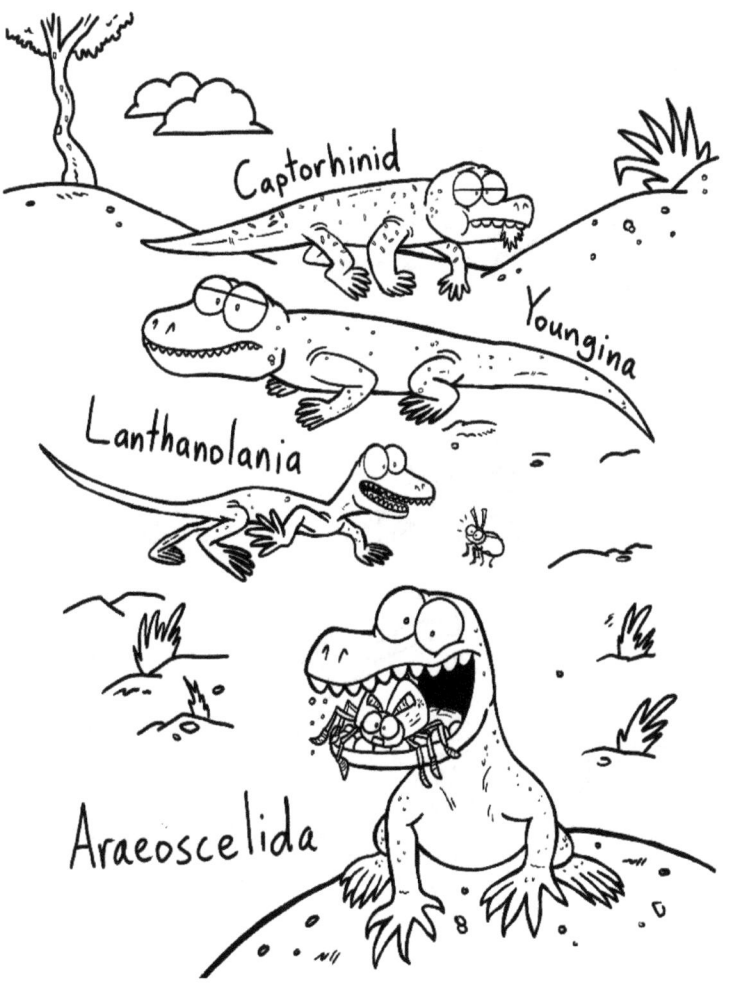

Captorhinid

Youngina

Lanthanolania

Araoscelida

And some even some spent their lives in and around the open seas…

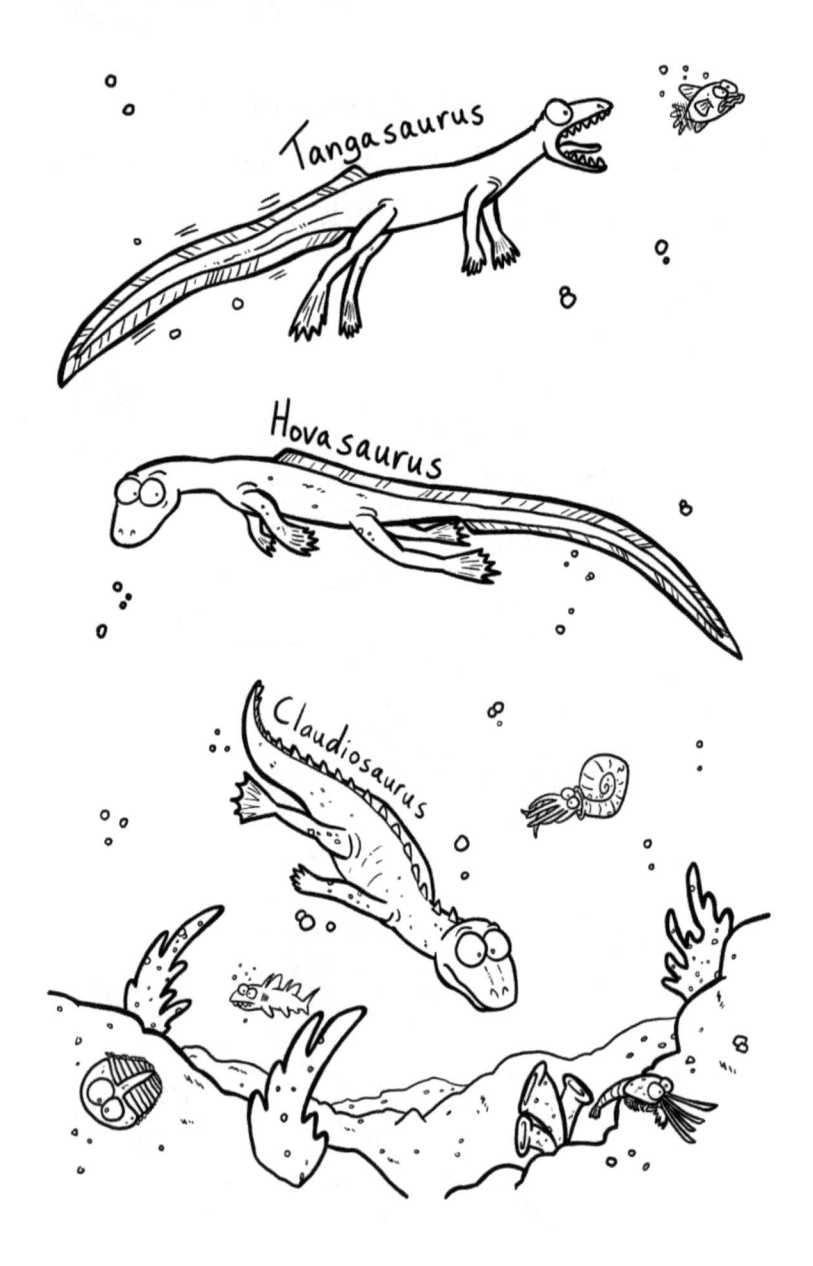

The Synapsids

During the Permian period, there were still lots of synapsids like the Edaphosaurs…

And the Ophiacodons.

There were also synapsids like Varanops. It was very fast land predator.

And it was a bit over a metre long (that's just over halfway up a door).

Sphenacodon was a big sail-backed predator in the Permian.

It was 3 metres long (that's almost as long as a whole car).

But the most famous Permian synapsid was Dimetrodon.

For the first half of the Permian period, Dimetrodon was the top predator.

It could hunt prey on land and in the shallow water.

And it could grow up to 4 and a half metres long (longer than a whole car).

But about 269 million years ago in the middle of the Permian a new type of synapsid evolved, they were the therapsids.

The Therapsids

One of the big ways the synapsids and therapsids were different was their legs. Synapsids had legs that stuck out the side and therapsids had legs that went down.

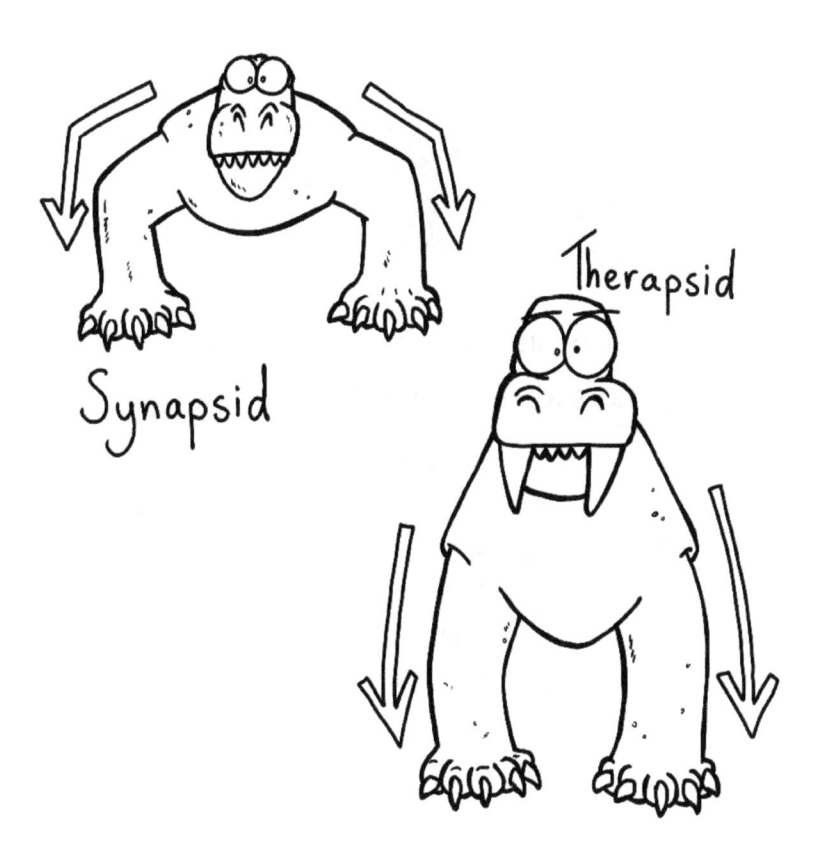

Synapsid

Therapsid

The earliest therapsid we know about is a little one called Biarmosuchus tener.

Biarmosuchus tener was a small land predator.

And it was about one and a half metres long (that's almost as tall as a door).

But over millions of years, lots of different therapsid shapes and sizes evolved…

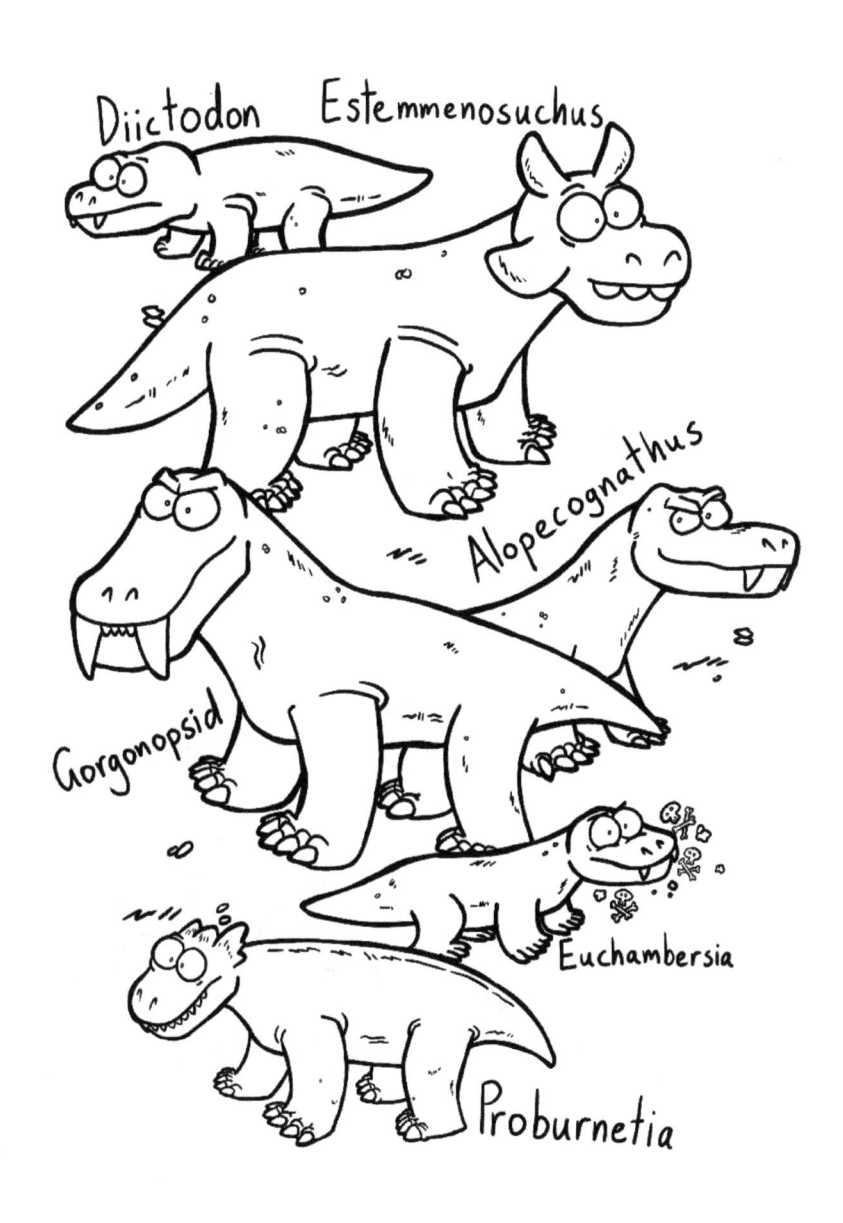

Diictodon

Estemmenosuchus

Alopecognathus

Gorgonopsid

Euchambersia

Proburnetia

Moschops was a plant-eating therapsid.

It was about 2 and a half metres long (over half a car length).

Estemmenosuchus ate plants and had a thick, bumpy skull.

And it was about 3 metres long.

The therapsid Jonkeria spent a lot of its time in water and ate both meat and plants.

And it could grow up to 5 metres long.

Galeops and Suminia were really small therapsids that ate plants…

And they were both about 50 centimetres long (almost two school rulers long).

Galeops probably lived in burrows underground.

And Suminia probably lived up in the trees.

There were lots of meat-eating therapsids that were about dog-sized with big snouts and fangs.

Lobalopex
Herpetoskylax
Lycaenodon
Burnetiidae
Hipposaurus
Pachydetes
Bullacephalus
Lophorhinus
Lemurosaurus
Ictidorhinus

Titanophoneus and Anteosaurus were the top predators around the middle of the Permian period.

And they were big, too. Anteosaurus was 6 metres long and Titanophoneus was 5 metres long (which makes them both a bit longer than a car).

Anteosaurus was a the top predator on land…

And in the shallow water, too.

Later in the Permian period, these new therapsids with saber-teeth took over as top predators. They were gorgonopsids.

Inostrancevia

Rubidgea

Sauroctonus

Eoarctops

Suchogorgon

When hunting, the gorgonopsids probably used their big teeth to bite something…

Then run away…

And wait for it to die so they could eat it.

This is Inostrancevia. It's the biggest gorgonopsid ever.

It was about 3 and a half metres long (almost a whole car length).

And this is Euchambersia. It's a pretty normal looking therapsid.

But what made this therapsid special is that it probably had a venomous bite…

And if that's true then it's the first ever vertebrate to have venom.

The End Permian Mass Extinction

Around 252 million years ago, a massive bulge of mantle pushed up through Earth's crust to the surface.

And burst through.

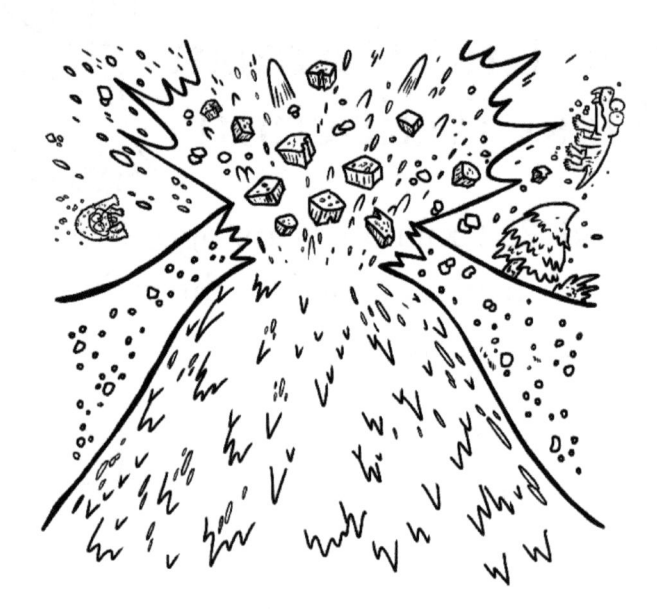

This caused a huge area to be covered in lava and erupting volcanoes.

The area of lava and volcanoes covered about 700 million square kilometres (that space is almost as big as the entire country of Australia).

This much lava caused Earth is to get a lot hotter with a lot more toxic gases…

And all that heat and toxic gases lasted for thousands of years…

The heat and toxic gases caused all the trilobites to finally go extinct...

And the eurypterids...

And even the spiny sharks.

In fact, so many animals went extinct that it was the worst mass extinction ever.

And hardly any animals were left when it was over.

The Permian period (and the entire Paleozoic era) was over, it was time for…

THE TRIASSIC PERIOD

But we'll learn about that period and more another time…

Living Things

Acanthostega: Devonian tetrapod

Acanthothoraci: Devonian placoderm

Acutiramus: Big Silurian eurypterid

Alopecognathus: Permian therapsid

Ammonoids: Devonian cephalopod

Amniotes: Tetrapod with hard eggs

Amphibamus: Carboniferous amphibian

Amphibians: Tetrapods, lay eggs in water

Anapsid: Have no extra skull holes

Andreolepis: Devonian ray-finned fish

Animals: Eukaryote with cells with lots of different jobs

Anomalocaris: Cambrian radiodont

Anteosaurus: Big Permian therapsid

Anthracosaurus: Carboniferous amphibian

Antiarchi: Devonian placoderm

Arachnids: Eight legged arthropod

Araeoscelida: Carboniferous sauropsid

Archaea: Really tough prokaryote

Archaeothyris: Carboniferous synapsid

Arthrodira: Devonian placoderm group

Arthropleura: Giant millipede

Arthropods: Hard outer-shelled animal

Astraspis: Ordovician ostracoderm

Australothyris: Permian parareptile

Bacteria: Prokaryote with endospores

Bactritoids: Devonian cephalopod

Bandringa: Carboniferous elasmobranch

Barameda: Carboniferous rhizodont

Biarmosuchus tener: Earliest therapsid

Bivalves: Mollusc with hinged-shell

Bony Fish: Fish with hard bone skeleton

Brachiopods: Mollusc with hinged-shell

Broomia: Permian parareptile

Bullacephalus: Dog-sized therapsid

Burnetiidae: Dog-sized therapsid

Captorhinid: Permian eureptile

Cartilaginous Fish: Fish with bendy bones

Caseodus: Carboniferous eugeneodont

Casineria: Carboniferous amniote

Cephalopods: Mollusc with tentacles

Charnia: Ediacaran filter feeder

Cheirolepis: Devonian ray-finned fish

Chordates: Animal with nerve chord

Claudiosaurus: Permian swimming eureptile

Coccosteus: Devonian placoderm

Coelacanth: Lobe-finned fish with extra fin

Coelurosauravus: Permian gliding parareptile

Conodonts: Little eel-shaped vertebrate

Cooksonia: First plant with roots

Coral: First evolved in Cambrian period

Crassigyrinus: Carboniferous amphibian

Crustacean: Arthropod with two antennae

Cyanobacteria: Prokaryote living in chains

Dendrerpeton: Carboniferous amphibian

Diapsid: Skull with two extra holes

Dickinsonia: Flat Ediacaran animal

Diictodon: Permian therapsid

Dimetrodon: Permian synapsid

Diplocaulus: Permian amphibian

Dunkleosteus: Big Devonian placoderm

Echinerpeton: Carboniferous synapsid

Echinoderms: symmetrical squishy life

Edaphosaurs: Plant eating synapsid

Edestus: Carboniferous eugeneodont

Elasmobranch: Stiff-finned cartilaginous fish

Endoceras: Biggest Ordovician nautiloid

Entelognathus: Silurian placoderm

Eoarctops: Permian gorgonopsid

Eryops: Permian amphibian

Estemmenosuchus: Permian therapsid

Euchambersia: Venomous therapsid

Euconcordia: Carboniferous sauropsid

Eudibamus: Permian parareptile on two legs

Eugeneodont: Ancient elasmobranch

Eukaryote: Have cells with a nucleus

Eunotosaurus: Permian parareptile

Eureptiles: Sauropsid skull with diapsid skull

Eurypterid: Arthropod with big claws

Eusthenopteron: Devonian tetrapodomorph

Fadenia: Carboniferous eugeneodont

Fanjingshania: Devonian cartilaginous fish

Fish: Vertebrate with gills

Fungus: Eukaryote that eats dead things

Gaiasaia: Permian big-fanged amphibian

Galeops: Permian burrowing therapsid

Gastropods: Mollusc with big curly shell

Gorgonopsids: Permian therapsid

Guiyu: Silurian, early bony fish

Haikouicthys: Cambrian chordate

Hallucigenia: Weird Cambrian animal

Helicoprion: Permian eugeneodont

Herpetoskylax: Dog-sized therapsid

Hipposaurus: Dog-sized therapsid

Hovasaurus: Permian swimming eureptile

Hybodonts: Spike-finned elasmobranch

Hylonomus: Earliest sauropsid

Hyneria: Carboniferous tetrapodomorph

Ichthyostega: Devonian tetrapod

Ictidorhinus: Dog-sized therapsid

Iniopterygiformes: Gliding elasmobranch

Inostrancevia: Biggest gorgonopsid ever

Jaekelopterus: Biggest eurypterid ever

Jellyfish: Wobbly animal with no brain

Jonkeria: Big Permian therapsid

Kimberella: Ediacaran squishy animal

Lancelet: Brainless chordate

Lanthanolania: Permian eureptile

Lanthanosuchoidea: Carboniferous sauropsid

Lemurosaurus: Dog-sized therapsid

Litoceras: Ordovician cephalopod

Lobalopex: Dog-sized therapsid

Lobe-Finned Fish: Fish with muscly fins

Lophorhinus: Dog-sized therapsid

Lungfish: Fish that can breathe air

Lycaenodon: Dog-sized therapsid

Macromerion: Carboniferous synapsid

Mesosaur: First parareptile in water

Metaspriggina: Cambrian, first fish

Microleter: Permian parareptile

Milleretta: Permian parareptile

Milleropsis: Permian parareptile

Millerosaurus: Permian parareptile

Millipedes: Arthropod with lots of legs

Molluscs: Have a mantle and no backbone

Nautiloids: Shelled cephalopod

Opabinia: Cambrian radiodont

Ophiacodon: Big carboniferous synapsid

Ophiderpeton: Carboniferous amphibian

Ornithoprion: Carboniferous eugeneodont

Osteostracans: Wide-headed ostracoderm

Ostracoderms: Fish with head shields

Pachydetes: Dog-sized therapsid

Paleothyris: Carboniferous sauropsid

Pambdelurion: Biggest Cambrian radiodont

Pandericthys: Devonian tetrapodomorph

Parareptiles: Sauropsid with anapsid skulls

Pareiasaurs: Big Permian parareptile

Pentecopterus: Big Ordovician eurypterid

Petalichthyidae: Devonian placoderm

Phoebodus: First elasmobranch

Phyllolepida: Small arthrodira

Pikaia: Cambrian chordate

Placoderms: Fish with bony plates on heads

Plathystrix: Permian amphibian

Plectronoceras: Earliest cephalopod

Prionosuchus: Biggest amphibian ever

Proburnetia: Permian therapsids

Prokaryote: Tiny blob with organelles

Proterogyrinus: Permian amphibian

Prototaxites: Huge fungus

Ptyctodontida: Devonian placoderm

Qianodus: Devonian cartilaginous fish

Qilinyu: Devonian placoderm

Radiodonts: Big Cambrian arthropod

Ray-Finned Fish: have hard bits in fins

Rhenanida: Devonian placoderm

Rhizodont: Carboniferous lobe-finned fish

Rhizodus: Biggest Rhizodont ever

Rolfosteus: Devonian arthrodira

Romerodus: Carboniferous eugeneodont

Rubidgea: Permian gorgonopsid

Sacambaspis: Ordovician ostracoderm

Saivodus: Carboniferous elasmobranch

Sauroctonus: Permian gorgonopsid

Sauropsids: Amniotes, diapsid or anapsid

Screbinodus: Carboniferous rhizodont

Sea Anemones: Cambrian squishy life

Silurolepis: Silurian placoderm

Sphenacodon: Permian synapsid

Spiny Sharks: Shark-shaped fish

Stethacanthus: Carboniferous elasmobranch

Strepsodus: Carboniferous rhizodont

Suchogorgon: Permian gorgonopsid

Suminia: Small Permian therapsid

Synapsids: Amniote with two-holed skull

Tangasaurus: Permian swimming eureptile

Tetrapodomorphs: Strong front-finned fish

Tetrapods: Four-legged animal

Therapsids: Straight-legged Permian synapsid

Tiktaalik: Carboniferous tetrapodomorph

Titanichthys: Huge Devonian placoderm

Titanophoneus: Big Permian therapsid

Trilobites: Flat-bodied arthropods

Tungsenia: Oldest tetrapodomorph

Tunicates: Blob- or tadpole-shaped chordate

Varanops: Permian synapsid

Vertebrates: Chordates with bones

Water Mites: Permian arthropods

Xenacanthids: Freshwater elasmobranch

Youngina: Permian eureptile

Books By David Conley

- That Book About Drawing Stuff
- That Book About Egyptian Mythology
- That Book About Greek Mythology
- The Book About Life Before Dinosaurs
- That Book About Norse Mythology
- That Book About Space Stuff
- That Activity Book About Greek Mythology
- That Activity Book About Norse Mythology
- That Activity Book About Egyptian Mythology

Coming Up!

Something new and exciting in 2025!

Stay tuned to find out!

About The Author

David Conley (a.k.a. David the Ferocious) was one of the most successful Vikings in history. He led many successful raids into playgrounds and fearlessly walked up the slippery dip as many times as he wanted and even rode a swing hands-free! David's career as a bloodthirsty Viking was cruelly cut short when he was attacked and killed by a rabid kindergartener.

David still loves to draw and write.

Find him on Instagram:

@thatdavidconley

Or just shoot him an email:
thatdavidconley@gmail.com